Also by Kim Nierman Smith

THE BOXED GARAGE

C O R N I C E Publishing
P. O. Box 657 Joshua Tree, CA 92252
kimniermansmith.com

ISBN (Paperback): 979-8-9868190-0-6
ISBN (Hardcover): 979-8-9868190-4-4
ISBN (Ebook): 979-8-9868190-2-0
Book design: Nuno Moreira, NMDESIGN

This book is a work of fiction. Names, characters, places and incidents either are products of the author's imagination or are used fictitiously. Any resemblance to actual events or locales or persons, living or dead, is entirely coincidental.

Park Parallel

Kim Nierman Smith

CORNICE Publishing

For Paul and Monty

Let's *GO*

INTRODUCTION

Every two weeks I checked on my mom. She was in her late eighties. I parked in the cul-de-sac, except for Tuesdays when the street sweeper came. Her car was kept in the garage. We had learned to drive together. She had been fifty-two and I fifteen. Each visit required a lengthy explanation of why her driver's license wasn't renewed after the stroke.

In an attempt to understand this new fractured reality, I assembled the fragments into poems.

Some of the poems are deeply personal, while others are more of a mystery, even to me.

STEPPING OFF

The water was murky
The depth was uncertain

Don't take things too personally
That's really hard
Living is a personal thing

Who knows

On the bed, questioning
Uh oh

Here goes

WARM SHIRT

Shapeless
Form full
Live and gone
Just now

RESILIENT DELICATES

The under rectangles
Chamomile carpet
That bird
Next day

THE FOLD

the back lays flat
bring the bottom up
left falls right
and right turns left
slide
flip the underneath
smooth
lift and throw

FRONDESCENCE

To have a green palm
is even better

YES AND NO

Sit
Unfold
Yawn
Clear throat
Sink in
Turn

Sunrise
Fold
Up

INTERVALS

Dulled memories
Slow Chirps
Bubble half blown
Sundown
Meld
Our time together

COLLECTIVE CARAVANSARY

get on get sleep get small get together get truth get creative get fear get fat get outside get through get real get nothing get vocal get vulnerable get tea get milk get fries get light get soap get happy get dog get inside get over get chocolate get everything get courage get off the wheel

LOOKING AT DEPARTURE

Waiting it
In the in between
Space and time
You're back mine
The murk
The muck
The mirror
Travel the parallel
horizontal wandering
Move on to you

CHAOS IN BEAUTY IN CHAOS

Octagon says go
Hello
Hello
Hello
Below the low is high
While rafting through the sky
I was stopped by a tree

FLAKY CRUST

Liberate your butter
The layers
will be happy
And make room for it

KNOT HERE

Slipped

on a frayed rope

Caught and
Pulled

on my end
on my edge

Walk on

Wits to the wall

Swing

BLOCK OF CLEAR

Accumulate
Dissipate

BULGE

d e f l a t e

It is again
What it was to be

The transparent solid

THE SPACE BETWEEN THE SPACE BETWEEN

That spot
that hollow

That spot
that day

That spot
is flat

WEEKDAYS WITH YOU

a wink a click
she's early

     a twist a glaze
     she's sugar

a snap a pinch
she's salty

     she's the sea

SIGNIFICANT

Asymmetric talk
paints inverted spaces
where light hits
and sun saves the day

R O U N D

There
There
and there

Here
Here
and there

There
There
and here

SOUL SHOW

Smiles
Patterns
Dimensions
Seed, Pit, Core
Me

WILD RELATIONS

Entangled easements

the push against
the pull arounds

We soak
We simmer
We stew

Under the over it

UN KNOWN

What's what's what?
What is ever
What is every
What is everything?

THE SMELL OF TIME

You passed by
      the dirt gave birth
you stopped

LITTLE WAXES

walk the room
to the thought
that the edge
does not exist
do in
undo
continue

IT'S LIKE

acquire attain buzz burn busy confusion Confucius dizzy daunting efficient
ethereal ecstatic flexible fluid glaze greed gullible head hazy harsh imagine
immoral impulsive judgement juice knee knuckle kiss liberate like lazy legal
mad magic naked noise now open organize other pause perfect persist
question quiet and ready

      surfing

                the

        cracks

WE ARE DIFFERENT
WE ARE THE SAME

I can fit into your things

It's comfort
for a time

until it's not
that comfortable

until it is

SWIMMING TO AFFINITY

Can the eyes be level
when the feet don't touch the bottom?

Orchestral blues

Upside down
can change the question

THE DIMENSION OF SOMEWHERE

Starry-eyed
still

Made plans
still

Cooked in the afternoon for the evening

Took a walk

and looked up
still

MAINTENANCE REQUIRED

The pants were sitting there
shade in the right places
Twisted Twills
       Emotional
              Unavailable

They liked sea and sand
a lot
and ate the sun
up and down
and were happy most of the time

THE SONG OF A TURTLENECK

It has storage
The cat likes it
and the hair makes it feel at home
It hibernates half the year
and is pampered like a lover

A CLEAN WELL EMPTIED REFRIGERATOR

There was butter

A green
A thing

starting to thaw

Two ends and no middle
One left
half eaten
Maybe order in again

BOX OF BUTS

Stay
Go
stay or go
The shelf was filled with them
As they stayed in place
and held on

PRESENT TENSE

Filling the shaker again today
and the grinder needs more ground

around the same time

today

Moving to the front and
starting from the back today

and again

starting the day

A CLOSE GROUP OF SPOTS

It's an assorted queue
of sun soaked spectacles
that never lose their attraction
Different shapes
of small
are caught in permanent conversation
Got lost in their curved world

SCREWED TOGETHER

The instructions were clear
we had to make sure all pieces
were lined up

The tools were included in the box

but there appeared to be a missing part

It was the holidays
and they were out of stock
until Spring

LIGHT WELL PLEASE

Looking for the exit
to the open here
An ant with a mission statement
on the collective mound
The distance is an illusion
and the mass is invisible

Going in

TOUCHING SHOULDERS

There were a few
next to each other
in the plastic drawer
showing signs of life

fine powdered

trying not to look vain

thinned skin

slight glistening

We all decompose

WHAT HAVE YOU DONE WITH THE SKY

senses check

check mood

cat check

check air

time check

check up

blank check

check check

SUCKING ON A NUANCE

Take the time to
see each layer
reveal the last
shade
flavor
smell
of personality
and then contemplate the center

WHEN BLOSSOMS HUM TOGETHER

I wasn't sure what to make of the heat and the wind
but the seeds were stage diving into a soiled ground

Shoulders were exposed
and envious smiles passed overgrown grasses

Salty smolder
See you soon

LISTEN TO YOUR TOSS

We exchange folded notes
in the afternoon
We sleep under the window sun
and our minds talk
We live a soft rectangle life
in the back of beyond

AN UNEVEN MOURNING

At the end of my fingers
there is your face
to connect the dots of time
A forest of shadows
lay down now
making a solid black
Close your eyes
and the gold spirit
will sprout

FOLLOW THE CRUMBS

Are they savory or sour
Did they come from familiar
Why should I trust them
Why wonder
Why wander
past the pavement

WEARING THE INSIDE OUT

Geometries
looking for edges
and finding none

Generalities
that touch

Cut the label off
Keep in a drawer

KIND MIRROR

What do you see
when you look at me

Me is we
and she
and he

It's a warm bulb

LOOSEN

Laid down to an ended day
and the beginning had just begun

CHOOSING SHAPES

Flying in a turbulent cruise phase
can feel indefinite in a heavy sky
Build the soft igloo
and land

PRETTY FEET

Crunch the sand
Bundle up
Fog

pit fires
puff clouds
polished

Speckles in ash
Dusted toes

Home

FULL OF OPEN

What now
When how
Where is the end of the edge
Why care

You are my foot
In the lengths

GREEN

A bath
An eye
A deep feeling
A shade place
Float on the bottom
Sink at the top
Night dust

HARD SWALLOW

Time does
As time does

It keeps

As we race to the end of ends
The pauses are what is missed
when the people mover stops

PEELING A HOT TOMATO

This protective film
to keep it all together
so we have control
Until it splits apart
and you just go with it
The sun made it's decision
It's my turn

MATTERS

It doesn't
Really
　　　In the middle
of two walls looking back
at themselves
in mirrored glasses
What happens between?

LOADING FLOW

The space, the gap
find the fit in
between the ears
That continuous marching band

                                           find the get out

between where and   there
surrounded by here

IT'S YOUR SERVE

A vertical wrinkle
is a laugh line

SUMMER'S MID

A half empty hourglass
will never know it's time

WILLFUL BARE

He wanted my attraction
but I had tasks
He was a distraction
from my tasks
He needed my attraction
so I had tasks
He was attracted
to my tasks
and I to him

BREVITY OF LONGING

Enter and slip
Return with forget
Repeat

CAN I ASK YOU SOMETHING

What is dread?
Can't breathe
Try
to answer the question

Background disappears
feeling e x p o s e d

RAISED BY MALLS

Pop music pretzels
Corn dogs
Perfect mass productions
move in a happy geometry
Pumped lips
Restless retailers
Fill up your sensory suitcases

SOPPING UP THE SADNESS

Stay in front of a smile
Make a joke
Leave the old air behind
and smell toasted oak
Walk puddles until
the walk is dry
and eyes close for the day

I FORGOT IT WAS YESTERDAY

Catching flies
and eating butter
The laughter threads
keep time now
Only a matter
of sequenced steps
hold real together

SAILING THIS SUBURB

Pantone floods the median
The hues stretch mindless
Saltwater pales
As it disappears into the sky
and night's black hole
takes oxygen away

WARMEST BLURS

Talking with cotton ears
Hard conversations are easy
A quiet upstairs window
Of translucent fog
Isn't open
Try again tomorrow
As if it was today

I'D RATHER BE BIRD WATCHING

Move to the curious side
and watch it fade away
until there's nothing to free

PATIENCE IS A VIRTUAL

The door is cracked

Open here

In between what's there and
not any more
There

It's slow now
and now
is what we
are
in

HOMES AND GARDENS

I look through my cypress wall
                    I see your cypress wall
Looking at me

OTHERED

Stay small
Lay on the floor
Same food
Today is the same

Under it
Stay a while

A shape on the wall
Planting time
Drawing the day
For minutes
Stay for a minute

THE UNDERWHELMS

Undefined mission
Undone faces
Unlikely outcome
of
the Unplanned

THE GRASSY FIELD

You want to hang out
Lay out
Kick a habit
crossing the coolness
Make out
Play underground
where the steam
makes sense

MOOD POOL

Working hard at
being a nicer person
on the outside

Soft center

Swimming with moths
in the shallow end
of the day

FORGETTING TO PRETEND

Pretending to forget

Tomorrow's story
believes yesterdays lyric

Skip

Scratch Scratch
Muddled scuttles
Tell me again
Two ideas

WHEN THE NEW TURNS

Noticing that book again

Adjust bottoms

Ice cream and strawberries

Why does paper yellow?

Sink in

Sand dunes and smoke

Sleeping in the afternoon

Wind picks up

Watermelon seeds

Ants

A CRACK FOR AIR

Breaking blue
under the overcast

Dusts catch light

Last pullover
this season

UNCONDITIONAL

Happily tasting the layers
of our frustration sandwiches

Moist with imprints
alongside the crust

Decided
Divided in half

Loose said so's
are fading
into the tablecloth

THE PROBLEM WITH LOOKING

Small feathers
and big plans

Ground is home
for now

Sky eyes
Street light travel

Hop
Hop

Wound up

CURVE THE CORD

In a room of pulleys
pick a ride
and life goes on

UNDOING UNDONE

Cutting up
the interior garden
until the natural light
is strung
New glasses
are always nice
to see through nonsense
on a sun cloud day

REVERSE CONTRACT

words
some getcaughtintheteeth
some flushed   out
blushed out

                                I'm out

another roundabout
route

MERGES AND CRUMBLES

A sliced minute
A speechless speckle
of a day
out in the neighborhood
every of every of every
out in the neighborhood
The street is slanted
and the sky
is ground

RECLUSIVE RECTANGLE

White tiles
Wet feet
Worried worriers
Warps
Wonder whys
Wonderful spider

Where is it?

THREE PILLOWS

Arranged
      and
changed and
arranged   to
change

LIQUID EYES

Throaty beats
Played it again

Senses and
seems
Dreams of
numbered scenes

Wherewithal's
What with what's

Backing in

INDEX

Life Skills Every Teen Girl Needs

Nurturing Resilience and Independence.
Growing Into a Confident Young Woman

Teen Empower

TABLE OF CONTENTS

INTRODUCTION

"I never dreamed about success. I worked for it." — **Estée Lauder**

T he wisdom of Estée Lauder truly encapsulates the journey that every young adult experiences during their formative years. Through perseverance, dedication, and developing crucial life skills, we come to understand that success is within reach and attainable.

Life can be challenging, and it's okay to feel uncertain when faced with difficulties. Success demands confidence and competence. It doesn't matter if you're shy, need help with career planning, or just want to live a healthy lifestyle. Everyone can benefit from guidance and improvement in certain areas. In this comprehensive guide, we will equip you with the necessary tools and knowledge to navigate the complexities of adulthood with confidence and competence. Whether you're a recent graduate embarking on a new journey in the professional world or simply seeking to enhance your life skills, this book is your go-to resource for mastering essential aspects of personal growth and success.

As you read through this book, you will discover numerous benefits that can enhance your life:

- Develop social skills, overcome shyness, and build meaningful connections
- Improve organization, time management, and productivity to achieve goals

- Learn to shop smart, create a balanced diet, and prepare budget-friendly meals

- Master home organization and DIY fixes for a calm and tidy living space

- Gain essential skills for managing finances, finding a job, and succeeding in interviews

- Prioritize self-care, establish boundaries, and cultivate personal growth and well-being

Throughout this book, we aim to equip you with the necessary knowledge and skills to navigate the challenges of adulthood with confidence and grace. Each chapter presents practical advice, actionable steps, and valuable insights that will empower you to thrive in all areas of your life.

So, get ready to embrace your inner boss and embark on a journey of personal growth and success!

CHAPTER 1

Breaking The Ice: Overcoming Shyness and Making New Friends

"Take advantage of every opportunity to practice your communication skills so that when important occasions arise, you will have the gift, the style, the sharpness, the clarity, and the emotions to affect other people ." - **Jim Rohn**

I f you are struggling with shyness, you may find it difficult to build meaningful relationships. However, there are effective strategies that can help you overcome shyness and connect with others. One important aspect is communication. Communication is essential in human interactions and forms the foundation of our social relationships. It provides people a way to relay information and express their ideas, thoughts, and feelings to one another. Effective communication is vital in almost all aspects of human life, especially in building personal, social, or work relationships. With good communication, conveying meaning or connecting with others would be easier. Here are some reasons why communication is essential:

Builds relationships: Communication is the foundation of any personal or professional relationship. It helps to create trust, attachment, and connection between individuals. Communication is a vital tool for building and maintaining relationships, as it helps us understand the needs and wants of others. It also allows us to express our own needs and wants. Good communication skills can lead to stronger, healthier relationships with family, friends, and colleagues.

Facilitates understanding and Learning: Effective communication allows people to understand each other's perspectives, needs, and concerns. It helps to prevent misunderstandings and conflicts. Disagreements, issues, and misunderstandings can arise when people have different opinions, expectations, and beliefs. Effective communication can resolve disputes by encouraging mutual understanding and finding solutions for everyone involved.

Communication is crucial to the learning process. Effective communication between teachers and students helps clarify concepts, build understanding, and promote active learning.

Increases productivity: Clear communication helps ensure everyone is on the same page, increasing efficiency, and productivity. It helps to minimize errors and wasted time. It also helps boost sales and improves customer satisfaction leading to high productivity and performance.

Effective communication can also boost employee motivation. Employees who feel heard and valued will likely do their best to attain their goals and improve performance levels.

Promotes personal and professional growth: Communication helps to exchange ideas and knowledge, which leads to personal and professional development. It enables individuals to learn from each other and develop new skills.

Communication provides opportunities to receive feedback from others. Constructive feedback helps identify areas needing improvement, allowing you to enhance skills and knowledge. You can pursue continuous learning and professional development by actively engaging in communication.

Enhances problem-solving: Communication is critical in business, where it is essential for sharing ideas, building relationships with customers, and negotiating deals. Communication, especially, plays a crucial role in problem-solving. It allows individuals to build customer relationships, identify issues, share their thoughts and ideas, and find solutions to problems.

Clear communication is crucial when implementing solutions. It ensures that those involved in problem-solving understand their roles, responsibilities, timelines, and expectations. Effective communication in all stages of implementation allows for adjustments, feedback, realignment, reinforcements, and continuous improvement.

Communication Skills Everyone Must Know

Good communication skills are essential in today's world, both in personal and professional contexts. Being able to effectively express oneself and understand others can make a significant difference in one's success and satisfaction in life.

Effective communication can help build strong relationships with colleagues and clients, convey ideas and information clearly, and resolve conflicts efficiently. Good communication skills can also enhance one's leadership abilities, as leaders must communicate their vision and expectations to their team.

It can also aid in expressing feelings and needs, leading to deeper and more fulfilling relationships.

Overall, having good communication skills can lead to more successful and satisfying personal and professional interactions, making it a crucial skill to acquire and continuously develop.

Types of Communication Skills

Here are some types of communication skills that everyone should know:

#1. Verbal Communication

Verbal communication is one of the primary types of communication used by humans and many other species. It involves using spoken words or vocalizations to convey information, express thoughts and feelings, and interact with others. It includes face-to-face conversations, phone calls, video chats, presentations, and speeches. Verbal communication allows for immediate feedback and clarification, facilitates understanding, and is the most common and direct way humans communicate with each other.

Here are some critical points about verbal communication:

Language: Verbal communication relies on using a shared language, which consists of a system of words, grammar, and rules for combining them. Different languages exist worldwide, enabling people to communicate within specific cultural and linguistic contexts.

Oral Expression: Verbal communication primarily occurs through speech. It involves the production of sounds and words using the vocal apparatus, including the tongue, lips, vocal cords, and other speech-related organs.

Information Transmission: Verbal communication enables the transfer of information from one person to another. It allows us to share knowledge, ideas, opinions, instructions, and experiences.

Real-Time Interaction: Verbal communication often occurs in real time, allowing immediate feedback and clarification. Conversations, discussions, and face-to-face interactions are common forms of verbal communication that facilitate real-time exchange.

Nuances and Context: Verbal communication conveys nuanced meaning through tone, emphasis, and intonation. Subtle pitch, volume, and emphasis changes can alter the intended message or emotional expression.

Limitations: Despite its effectiveness, verbal communication has certain restrictions. Misinterpretation, miscommunication, and misunderstandings can occur due to differences in language proficiency, cultural context, accents, or other factors. Additionally, verbal communication requires the presence of both parties at the same time and place, limiting its reach in certain situations.

Verbal communication plays a crucial role in human interaction. It is a fundamental aspect of everyday life, enabling individuals to connect, share knowledge, express emotions, and build relationships.

#2. Written Communication

This form of communication includes text messages, emails, letters, reports, and other written documents that rely on language to convey information and ideas.

Effective written communication is essential in many contexts. Good writing should be clear, concise, and well-organized, focusing on the intended audience and purpose. It should also be free of grammar, spelling, and punctuation errors, as these can detract from the message.

Writing can be formal or informal, and the tone and style will depend on the context and purpose of the communication. For example, a business report might use a more formal tone and structure, while a personal email might be more informal and conversational.

In today's digital age, written communication has become even more prevalent due to the widespread use of email, instant messaging, and social media platforms. These forms of writing require different skills and strategies than traditional writing. They may also have different rules and expectations around language use. However, regardless of the medium, the principles of effective written communication remain the same: clarity, coherence, and consideration for the audience.

Overall, effective written communication is a crucial skill for success and requires practice, attention to detail, plus an understanding of the audience and the purpose of the communication.

#3. Active Listening

Paying close attention to the speaker to understand the message is active listening. It is the ability to fully concentrate on what someone is saying without interrupting and responding appropriately. It is never enough to listen to the speaker's words but also take note of their tone of voice, body language, and overall message while providing feedback to the speaker that they are being heard and understood.

Active listening requires your entire presence and engagement in the conversation without distractions or interruptions. It also shows empathy and respect for the speaker's feelings and perspectives, even if the listener disagrees.

Active listening is vital in personal and professional relationships, as it helps to build trust, improve communication, and resolve conflicts more effectively.

#4. Nonverbal Communication

Nonverbal communication refers to using body language, facial expressions, tone of voice, gestures, and other nonverbal cues to convey the meaning of words spoken. It is an essential component of practical communication skills and can significantly impact the success of any conversation or interaction.

Some examples of nonverbal communication include:

Eye contact: Maintaining eye contact with the speaker can show interest and engagement.

Facial expressions: Smiling or frowning can convey emotions and attitudes toward the conversation.

The tone of voice: voice tone can indicate the speaker's emotional state, such as anger or happiness.

Posture: How a person sits, or stands can indicate confidence or nervousness.

Gestures: Hand movements or body language can emphasize points, show agreement or disagreement, or convey enthusiasm.

In summary, nonverbal communication can significantly enhance or detract from the effectiveness of communication skills. Being aware of one's nonverbal cues and reading the nonverbal cues of others can help improve communication and create more positive and productive interactions.

#5. Assertive Communication

You are assertive means expressing your thoughts and opinions clearly and confidently without being aggressive or disrespectful.

Assertiveness is a communication skill that involves expressing your thoughts, feelings and needs directly and respectfully. It involves standing up for yourself without being aggressive or passive. To be assertive in your communication:

Use "I" statements: Start your sentences with "I" to express your thoughts and feelings directly. It is easy to take responsibility for your message and avoid blaming others.

Be clear and specific: Clearly and expressly state what you want or need. Use concrete examples to make your point.

Use a confident tone: Use a confident tone of voice to convey your message. Avoid sounding apologetic or unsure.

Respect others: Be respectful to the other person's feelings and needs. Avoid using aggressive language or attacking the other person.

Practice active listening: Listen actively to the other person's response. Summarize and simplify their words to show that you understand their perspective.

Offer solutions: Offer solutions or alternatives when possible. It can help to find a compromise that works for both parties.

Stand your ground: Don't back down if the other person tries to bully or manipulate you. Stay calm and assertive in your communication.

Remember, being assertive is not about being aggressive or confrontational. It's about expressing yourself clearly and respectfully while respecting your rights and needs.

#6. Negotiation and Persuasion Communication

Negotiation and persuasion are essential communication skills in everyday interactions, business, personal relationships, and politics. Both techniques involve influencing others to adopt a particular viewpoint, reach a mutually beneficial agreement, or take a specific action. While negotiation focuses on finding common ground and compromising, persuasion aims to convince others to accept a particular position or idea.

Conflict resolution is part of negotiation and persuasion involving managing and resolving conflicts constructively. Here are ways to resolve disputes effectively:

Stay calm: It's essential to stay calm during a conflict. Keep your emotions under control to think clearly and positively. You can make better decisions and respond productively without those negative emotions.

Listen actively: Listen actively to the other person's perspective. There are many angles to every point. To understand theirs, try asking questions to clarify any misunderstandings.

Find common ground: Try finding areas of agreement and find common ground. It can help to build a foundation for resolving the conflict.

Brainstorm solutions: Work together to brainstorm solutions that can meet the needs of both parties. Be open to compromise and creative solutions.

Agree on a solution: To solve an issue; you must reach an agreement and make sure that the solution is put into action.

Follow up: Follow up on the solution to ensure it works effectively. Make adjustments if necessary and continue to communicate openly to prevent future conflicts.

Conflict resolution is about finding a solution that respectfully and constructively meets both parties' needs and not about winning or losing. You can effectively resolve conflicts and build stronger relationships by practicing good communication skills, active listening, and a willingness to compromise.

#7. Cross-Cultural Communication

Awareness of cultural differences and adapting your communication style can prevent misunderstandings and promote effective communication.

Cultural awareness is an essential communication skill that involves understanding and respecting cultural differences. There are ways to improve your cross-cultural awareness. Here are some of them.

Avoid stereotypes: Avoid making assumptions or generalizations about people based on their culture, ethnicity, or background.

Study about different cultures: Take the time to learn about other cultures and their customs. It can help you to understand better and respect cultural differences.

Be open-minded: Accepting other cultural differences is easy when you are open to different perspectives.

Use appropriate language: Use language suitable and respectful of different cultures. Do not use offensive language or refrain from making jokes that could offend others.

Respect personal space: Different cultures have different norms regarding personal space. Respect personal freedom and avoid invading someone's personal space without their consent.

Show interest in other cultures: Show an interest in different cultures and ask questions to learn more. It can help to build a deeper understanding and appreciation of cultural differences.

Be patient: Be patient when communicating with people from different cultures. Allow for more time to speak and be willing to explain things more than once.

Being culturally aware in your communication is about respecting different cultures and being willing to learn and understand cultural differences. By practicing good communication skills and showing an interest in other cultures, you can build stronger relationships with people from different backgrounds.

#8.Presentation Skills (Visual Communication Skills)

Presenting information clearly, and engagingly is essential in any professional and academic field.

Presentation skills are an essential component of effective communication. No matter how many people you are presenting to, your ability to convey the message clearly and persuasively can significantly impact the success of your communication.

Take these critical factors into consideration to have a more effective presentation.

Clarity: A good presentation is clear and concise. Do not use jargon or technical words to make your message easy to understand and reach your audience. These words could be confusing if they aren't familiar with them.

Organization: A well-organized presentation will help your audience follow your message and stay engaged. It's best to outline to organize your thoughts and ideas and make sure your presentation flows well.

Visual aids: If you want your message to be more engaging, use visual aids. They can reinforce them. Make sure your visual aids are straightforward and clearly understood by your audience.

Delivery: When delivering your presentation, speak clearly and confidently. The way you talk can be as vital as your presentation. Use eye contact body language to engage your audience and emphasize key points.

Engagement: Keeping your audience engaged and interested is essential for a successful presentation. Encourage participation through interactive elements such as asking questions or taking polls.

Overall, practical presentation skills require clear communication, thoughtful organization, engaging delivery, and creative use of visual aids. With practice and preparation, anyone can improve their presentation skills and communicate more effectively.

How to Practice Good Communication

Tips and different ways to improve your ability to communicate with others:

Be open-minded: Be open to different perspectives and be willing to consider other viewpoints.

Ask questions: Ask questions to clarify understanding and to show that you are actively listening.

Read widely and keep learning: Reading can help you develop your vocabulary and improve your ability to express yourself clearly and effectively. Keep learning about new communication techniques and strategies.

Be patient: Be patient. Take your time to communicate clearly and effectively.

Use examples and stories: Stories and real-world examples can make your message more engaging, and draw illustrations for your points so your audience can visualize them.

Practice consistently: The more you practice your communication skills, the more confident and effective you will become.

Seek feedback: Ask people for feedback. You will know which areas to improve the next time you give your message. Feedback is for improvement and must be taken as constructive criticism.

Be clear and concise: Clarity and conciseness are essential to practical communication skills. Being clear and concise in your communication helps ensure that your message is understood. Clarity means expressing oneself clearly and accurately without ambiguity or confusion. It involves using appropriate vocabulary, grammar, and tone and organizing ideas logically and coherently.

Conversely, conciseness refers to the ability to convey information succinctly and efficiently without unnecessary elaboration or wordiness. It involves using only the essential words and phrases to relay the message while avoiding redundancy or repetition.

Together, clarity and conciseness help ensure that communication is effective and efficient. By expressing oneself clearly and succinctly, one can avoid misunderstandings and ensure the intended message is received and understood. Clarity and conciseness are often critical to achieving one's goals and objectives in professional settings.

Use Respectful Language: Avoid offending people with your language. Respect and consideration for others to create a positive and productive conversation with others. To ensure you know how to use respectful language, here are some tips:

Use appropriate titles and honorifics: Addressing someone by their proper title and using honorifics like "Mr.", "Mrs.", "Ms.", or "Dr." shows respect for their status and achievements.

Avoid offensive language: Avoid using language that may offend someone based on race, ethnicity, gender, religion, or sexual orientation.

Listen attentively: Show that you respect the other person's opinion by actively listening to them. Avoid interrupting them and try to understand their perspective.

Use polite phrases:

- Use polite words like "please."

- "Thank you."
- "Excuse me" to show respect and appreciation.

Be mindful of tone: Your voice can convey a lot of information. Ensure that your tone sounds respectful and just right for the situation.

Use inclusive language: Use language inclusive of all genders, races, and cultures. Avoid making assumptions about someone's identity.

Be mindful of nonverbal communication: Body language can convey much information. Make sure that your nonverbal communication is respectful and appropriate for the situation.

Overall, using respectful language in communication is essential to building positive relationships and creating a productive conversation.

Exercise Empathy: Understanding and being able to relate to the emotions and feelings of others is crucial in effective communication. It is an essential component of practical communication skills as it allows people to connect on a deeper level and build stronger relationships.

In communication, empathy involves:

- Actively listening to the other person.
- Putting oneself in their shoes.
- Trying to understand their perspective and feelings.

It involves being present in the conversation, avoiding judgment or assumptions, and acknowledging the other person's emotions and experiences.

Here are some ways in which empathy can improve communication skills:

- It builds trust: When people feel heard and understood, they will likely trust the person they are communicating with.

- It reduces conflict: When people feel that their perspective is acknowledged and respected, they are less likely to become defensive or argumentative.

- It promotes collaboration: When people understand each other's perspectives, they can work together more effectively to achieve a common goal.

- It enhances relationships: Empathy helps create more meaningful and authentic connections between people, leading to stronger relationships.

In short, empathy is an essential skill in communication as it allows people to connect on a deeper level, build stronger relationships, and achieve better outcomes in their interactions.

Improving your communication skills requires time and effort, but the benefits are worth it. Becoming a better communicator can enhance your personal and professional relationships, build trust and respect, and achieve your goals more effectively.

When communication is done well, it can help avoid misunderstandings, resolve conflicts, and foster collaboration and understanding. Therefore, it is crucial to develop good communication skills to improve the quality of your interactions with others and achieve your goals.

How to Build Rapport and Make a Positive First Impression

Building good rapport and making a good first impression through communication can be achieved through several strategies.

How to Build Rapport

Building rapport with others is an essential first step in developing meaningful friendships. Here are strategies on how to do so through communication:

Show genuine interest: To show others that you are interested in them, ask them about their ideas, life, and interests. Actively listen to their answers. Make comments from time to time or follow up with further questions. It will show you that you are genuinely interested in the conversation.

Be cheerful and friendly: Smile, use open body language, and maintain eye contact to convey a welcoming and approachable demeanor. Share your experiences and thoughts to create a positive and uplifting atmosphere.

Find shared interest: Look for shared interests or experiences you can bond over. Whether it's a love for a particular band, a favorite hobby, or a shared experience, finding common ground can help establish a connection.

Practice active listening: When listening, focus entirely on the speaker and avoid interrupting or finishing their sentences. Show interest in the topic by nodding, making eye contact, and providing verbal cues such as "uh-huh" or "I see."

Be yourself: Authenticity is critical in building lasting friendships. Don't try to be someone you're not or pretend to like something to impress someone. Be genuine, and you'll attract people who appreciate and connect with you for who you indeed are.

Building rapport takes time and effort, so be patient and persistent.

How to Make a Good First Impression

An excellent first impression is lasting and crucial in many social and professional situations. There are ways you can do to create a positive first impression:

Dress appropriately: Wear clothing that is appropriate for the occasion and fits well. Your outfit should be clean, neat, and in good condition.

Be punctual: Arrive on time or even a few minutes early. Tardiness can create a negative impression, especially on a first meeting. It suggests you don't respect the other person's time.

Smile and have eye contact: Eye contact is essential when meeting someone. With a friendly smile, it shows that you are friendly and approachable. It also makes them feel at ease as they can sense that you are interested in what they say.

Use their names: People love to be called their names. It gives a sense of identity. Addressing someone by their name can make them feel valued and important and make them comfortable and at ease talking to you.

Be polite: Get into the habit of saying "please" and "thank you" when communicating. Polite language and manners speak a lot about you. Also, avoid interrupting or talking over others.

Ask questions: You can be straightforward if you want to know more about a person. Ask him questions that tell more about them to show your interest. Conversing with them shows that you are interested in what they say.

Be positive: People are naturally attracted to positive energy. Try to stay optimistic during your conversation.

Show empathy: Showing empathy can help you build a stronger connection with the other person.

Be authentic: Finally, be yourself. Anyone can quickly sense when someone is not sincere. Being authentic and genuine can help you build strong connections with people and establish trust.

Listen actively: Listening is critical to building good rapport. When talking to someone, listen attentively. Show enthusiasm for the conversation or activity you are engaged in. It can create a positive and engaging atmosphere.

Remember, making an excellent first impression is not about being fake or insincere but about showing respect and interest for the other person.

How to Make Friends

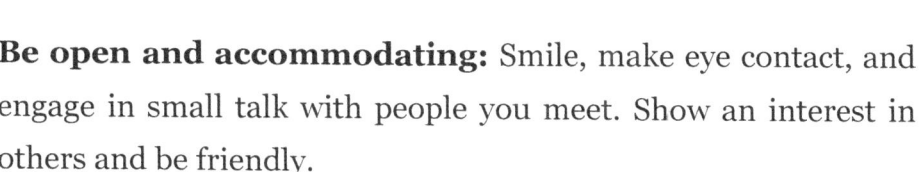

Making friends can seem daunting, but with the right mentality and approach, it can be a fulfilling experience. Here are ways on how to make friends:

Be open and accommodating: Smile, make eye contact, and engage in small talk with people you meet. Show an interest in others and be friendly.

Join clubs or groups: Consider joining a club or group that interests you. These places are a good start if you want to meet new friends or acquaintances who share your hobbies or interests. They exist for a common purpose. You can also volunteer your service to do something good for your community. Seek volunteer opportunities in your area and stand for a cause.

Attend social events like parties, barbecues, or community events. Be sure to introduce yourself and strike up conversations with new people.

Use social media: When looking for new connections, social media can help you find new friends who share your interests. Join groups or communities related to your hobbies or passions, and converse with others.

Be yourself: Don't try to be someone you're not to fit in. Be authentic to yourself, and you'll attract people who appreciate you for who you are.

Making friends takes time and effort, so be patient and keep trying. Don't be discouraged if you don't hit it off with everyone you meet – sometimes, finding the right people who will become good friends takes time.

How to Choose Your Friends Wisely

Wisely choosing when selecting your friends is essential to maintaining positive relationships. Consider these ways to choose your friends wisely:

Consider your values: Consider what values are important to you and seek out people who share those same values. Be sure that you and your friends share the same priorities. These values include trustworthiness, loyalty, authenticity, respect, etc.

Observe their behavior: Pay attention to how your potential friends treat others, especially those who are different. Being respectful and kind to everyone is a good sign that they are empathetic and accepting.

Look for common interests: Finding people with similar interests can help you build meaningful connections. It's more enjoyable and productive when you share your passions and hobbies with more likely interested people.

Consider their attitude: Surrounding yourself with positive people can positively impact your mood and outlook. Look for optimistic, supportive friends who encourage you to be your best self.

Trust your instinct: Some people call it gut, but if something feels off about a potential friend, listen to your instincts. Your intuition can guide you toward the people who will be your life's most positive and uplifting influences.

Remember that building strong friendships takes time, effort, and mutual respect. Pick the right people to spend time with, and you can create a supportive and fulfilling social network that enriches your life.

Body Language

Body language is the nonverbal cues and signals to communicate their ideas, feelings, thoughts, and intentions. It involves using various physical cues, such as facial expressions, gestures, postures, and eye movements, to convey a message or express oneself.

Body language is essential to human communication, as it can often convey more meaning than spoken words. It serves as a tool to express emotions, attitudes, intentions, and offers insights into a person's thoughts and feelings. People can better understand what others think and feel by paying attention to body language cues and adjusting their communication accordingly.

Types of Body Language

Body language refers to the nonverbal communication we express through physical gestures, posture, facial expressions, and eye contact. Here are some common types of body language:

Facial expressions - use facial expressions to communicate emotions, such as smiling, raising eyebrows, frowning, sulking, raising eyebrows, or squinting.

Posture - How we sit or stand unknowingly communicates our confidence, power, or shyness to others. Examples include standing tall, slouching, leaning forward, or crossing arms.

Gestures - hand and arm movements can express emotions, indicate agreement or disagreement, or signal directions. Examples include nodding, shaking the head, pointing, or waving.

Eye contact - maintaining eye contact can show interest or confidence while avoiding eye contact can indicate discomfort or deceit.

Touch - communication can communicate emotions, such as affection, aggression, or comfort. Examples include hugging, shaking hands, patting someone on the back, or pushing someone away.

The tone of voice - how we speak, including our pitch, volume, and inflection, can communicate emotions and attitudes. For example, shouting conveys anger or excitement, while a soft tone suggests vulnerability or calmness.

Microexpressions - brief, involuntary facial expressions that can reveal underlying emotions, such as surprise, fear, or disgust.

Understanding and interpreting body language can be essential in many situations, such as job interviews, negotiations, or social interactions.

How to Read Body Language

Reading body language is a skill that helps you analyze a person's noncommunication signals and cues, enabling you to understand what they are feeling or thinking without the need to say them explicitly. Consider these tips to help you read body language:

Pay close attention to facial expressions: An individual's facial expressions can reveal much about someone's feelings. Look for cues such as raised eyebrows, wrinkled forehead, and smiles or frowns.

Observe body posture: How someone stands, or sits can indicate their confidence, interest, or discomfort level. For example, someone hunched over may feel anxious or unsure.

Pay attention to eye contact: Eye contact can convey interest, awareness, or dishonesty. Someone who avoids eye connection may be feeling nervous or untruthful.

Listen to tone of voice: Someone's voice can reveal their emotional state. For example, a monotone voice may indicate boredom or disinterest, while a high-pitched voice may indicate excitement or nervousness.

Notice gestures: Gestures such as hand movements or leaning forward can reveal someone's level of engagement in a conversation. For example, someone who is fidgeting may be feeling uncomfortable or restless.

Consider the context: Body language can vary depending on the situation. Consider the environment, the people involved, and any cultural differences that may impact someone's body language.

Remember that reading body language is not an exact science. It should be used to complement other forms of communication to gain a complete understanding of what someone is feeling or thinking.

How to Read Facial Expressions

Reading facial expressions can be valuable in many settings, from personal relationships to professional interactions. It involves observing the subtle changes in a person's face to gain insight into their emotions, thoughts, and intentions. The following are steps to help you read facial expressions:

Learn the basics: Seven universal facial expressions are recognized across cultures: happiness, anger, fear, disgust, surprise, contempt, and sadness. Please familiarize yourself with these expressions to recognize them when you see them.

Please pay attention to the person's eyes: They reveal a lot about their emotions and are considered the windows to the soul. Look for changes in pupil size, blinking rate, and gaze direction to get clues about how the person feels.

Observe the mouth and lips: The mouth can tell how a person feels. Notice any changes in the position of the lips, in the shape of the mouth, and any movements, such as smiling or frowning.

Look at the eyebrows: The position and movement of the eyebrows can indicate surprise, anger, or confusion. When someone raises their eyebrows, it could mean they are surprised or curious. At the same time, furrowed brows could indicate confusion or anger.

Pay attention to other facial features: Other facial features, such as the nose, cheeks, and forehead, can also provide information about a person's emotional state. For example, a flushed face could indicate embarrassment or anger.

Be observant of microexpressions: Microexpressions are brief, involuntary facial expressions that reveal someone's hidden emotions no matter how much they hide them. These expressions are often fleeting and difficult to spot, but you can learn to recognize them with practice.

Consider the context: Facial expressions can be influenced by many factors, including cultural norms, individual personality traits, and the specific situation or context. The context of the situation is significant when interpreting facial expressions, so always consider it. The same facial expression can have different meanings depending on the situation and the person's cultural background. For example, a person who suffered tremendously from betrayal may not display as much emotion on their face as someone who has not experienced it.

Practice empathy: When trying to read someone's facial expressions, putting yourself in their shoes is essential. This way, you can imagine what they might be feeling. It can help you to interpret their expressions better and respond appropriately.

Seek feedback: Reading body language is often inaccurate, especially when you're just beginning to learn the skill. Ask for feedback on your ability to read facial expressions from other people. You will be able to identify points you need to improve your craft.

Consistently practice: Reading facial expressions takes an approach, so try to pay attention to the faces of those around you and practice reading their nonverbal communication cues. You can also use online resources or take classes to improve your skills.

In reading facial expressions, there's always a chance for misinterpretation. However, with practice and observation, you can become more skilled at recognizing and interpreting facial expressions. Also, it's essential to approach this skill with sensitivity and empathy.

While improving communication skills and making friends may seem like two different topics, they are closely related. One of the critical components of building solid relationships is effective communication, which involves expressing oneself clearly and actively listening and understanding the other person. You can make new friends and deepen existing relationships by honing your communication skills. In the next chapter, we will tackle the importance of executive functions.

CHAPTER 2

How to Plan Like a Boss: Strategies for Outsmarting Your Future Self

---

"Lack of direction, not lack of time, is the problem. We all have twenty-four hour days."

—Zig Ziglar

P lanning like a pro means taking a dynamic approach to managing your time, resources, and goals. It involves various skills, such as anticipating obstacles and opportunities, setting priorities, and developing a clear action plan.

To outsmart your future self, you must create strategies considering your strengths, weaknesses, tendencies, and external factors that can impact your success. By adopting a growth mindset and staying focused on your goals, you can become a master planner and achieve your desired outcomes.

Executive Functioning Skills

Executive functioning pertains to cognitive skills responsible for goal-directed behavior, problem-solving, decision-making, and self-regulation.

Strong executive functioning skills empower individuals to live, work, and learn independently and competently, equipping them with the capacity to obtain, analyze, and execute information and solutions.

Executive functioning abilities encompass various cognitive skills, which may include:

Selective Attention: Paying attention to relevant visual, auditory, and sensory information while ignoring irrelevant stimuli.

Example: When students with high selective attention skills study in a coffee shop, they can tune out the noise and focus on their studies. On the other hand, someone with poor selective attention will find it hard to concentrate and easily get distracted by the environment's noise and stimuli.

Organization: Arranging one's environment or schedule systematically and structure to improve efficiency and productivity.

Example: When juggling multiple tasks, a student with solid organization skills will create a to-do checklist, prioritize projects based on their due dates, and break down the tasks into manageable chunks to ensure they complete everything on time.

Inhibitory Control: Suppressing impulses and resisting the urge to engage in impulsive behaviors that may violate social expectations and norms.

Example: Imagine you're in a quiet movie theater, and your phone rings loudly. If you have inhibitory solid control skills, you can resist the urge to answer your phone and instead silence it or step outside to take the call. Doing so allows you to follow the social norm of not disturbing others in a quiet environment.

Planning: Formulating a course of action or strategy to achieve a specific goal or outcome.

Example: Let's say you have a big school project coming up, like a research paper or presentation. With good planning skills, you'll start by breaking the project into smaller, more manageable parts. You can create a schedule for researching and writing, set deadlines for each, and plan how to use your time each day. By doing this, you'll be able to stay on track and avoid feeling overwhelmed.

Working Memory: Holding and manipulating information in one's mind briefly to perform cognitive tasks effectively.

Example: If your teacher asks you to solve a math problem, you'll need to remember the numbers and calculations as you work through the issue. Using your working memory effectively allows you to hold and manipulate this information in your mind long enough to solve the problem correctly.

Decision-making: Analyzing possible options and their potential outcomes to make informed and effective choices.

Example: If you have good decision-making skills, you'll start considering each option's pros and cons. You begin to think about which activity you enjoy more, which will help you achieve your goals, and which fits better with your schedule. By analyzing your options carefully, you'll be able to make an informed and practical choice you'll be happy with.

Time Management: Estimating the time and effort required in completing a task and prioritizing activities based on their importance and urgency.

Example: Let's say you have a project due in a week and other homework and activities. With good time management skills, you'll begin by outlining how much time you need for each task. You may start with the project because it's the most important and has a deadline. Then, you'll plan specific times to work on it during the week. You'll also make sure to fit in time for your other homework and activities, but you'll do them based on what's essential and urgent.

Initiation: Starting and executing tasks or actions required to achieve a desired outcome.

Example: Students who have projects to complete may feel suppressed and need help figuring out where to start. However, by creating a plan and taking the first step, such as conducting research or outlining their ideas, they are initiating the task and setting themselves on the path to achieving their desired outcome.

All these skills mentioned above are critical for your academic and social success as they facilitate crucial skills and behavior that can affect your problem-solving, goal-setting, and decision-making abilities.

Now, that's a long list of skills! What's astounding is that most of us use these skills without realizing it. Our brain does it automatically and quickly without us having to overthink. However, some people may need help with these skills and extra help to improve.

Importance of Executive Functioning Skills

Executive functioning is crucial for various aspects of our daily lives. Here are some key reasons why executive functioning is essential:

1. **Goal setting and planning:** Executive functioning allows us to set goals, develop strategies, and plan the steps needed to achieve those goals. It helps us prioritize tasks, organize thoughts, and create effective action plans.

2. **Impulse control and self-regulation:** Executive functioning helps us manage impulses, resist distractions, and control our emotions. It enables us to think before acting, make thoughtful decisions, and regulate our behavior appropriately.

3. **Attention and focus:** Executive functioning supports our ability to concentrate, sustain attention, and filter out distractions. It allows us to stay focused on tasks, ignore irrelevant information, and switch between tasks efficiently.

4. **Problem-solving and decision-making:** Executive functioning skills facilitate effective problem-solving by enabling us to analyze situations, generate solutions, and make informed decisions. It helps us consider different perspectives, evaluate alternatives, and anticipate potential consequences.

5. **Flexibility and adaptability:** Executive functioning allows us to adapt to new situations, switch gears when necessary, and adjust our strategies. It helps us think flexibly, adapt to changes, and overcome obstacles.

6. **Time management and organization:** Executive functioning is crucial in managing time effectively, setting priorities, and organizing tasks. It helps us allocate time wisely, meet deadlines, and maintain a structured approach to work and life.

7. **Working memory:** Executive functioning supports working memory, which is essential for holding and manipulating information in our mind. It allows us to follow instructions, remember details, and integrate new information with existing knowledge.

Strong executive functioning skills contribute to improved productivity, problem-solving abilities, decision-making, self-control, and overall success in various aspects of life, including academics, work, relationships, and personal well-being.

Planning

What is Planning?

Planning is a skill that helps us get things done in the future. It involves figuring out what we need to do, making a plan, and breaking it down into smaller steps.

Planning is vital because it helps us organize our thoughts and resources to achieve our goals. It's like putting together a puzzle—we need to have all the right pieces and put them in the proper sequence or position to solve the problem.

On the other hand, lack of planning limits our success despite having good intentions. There are many reasons for this, including taking unnecessary actions, missing relevant measures, and needing to be more efficient. Without a plan, we may have to redo projects, assignments, and other essential matters. In short, we waste time, opportunities, and valuable resources.

When we plan, we figure out how to do something step-by-step. Here are some examples of planning behaviors that can help us get things done:

- Knowing what order to do things in
- Having a particular spot or space for items we need
- Having a plan for specific activities
- Making a plan for doing a lot of things
- Using tools like calendars or planners to help us remember what to do

Honing your planning skills will help you succeed in different aspects of your life. Experts believe that planning and organizing skills help with the following:

- Doing better in school and feeling good about their achievements
- Having good relationships with family and friends
- Doing well in jobs and careers later in life

How to Plan Effectively

Effective planning involves breaking down a bigger goal into smaller, more manageable steps. It also means thinking ahead, identifying potential challenges or roadblocks, and then developing a plan to overcome them.

When you plan effectively, you are more likely to succeed and feel accomplished in what you set out to do. So, where do you start?

Step #1: Write Down Your Goal

Often, we set goals because someone else wants us to or we think it's what we should do. But to achieve a goal, choosing something you genuinely want for yourself is crucial.

Take some time for self-reflection to decide on a goal aligning with your values and desires. Write it down if you must, as this will help you remain motivated and committed to achieving it. Remember to utilize the SMART formula:

Specific: This means being clear about what you want to achieve and how you should execute the plan. When setting a goal, consider: who, what, when, where, and why.

Measurable: How will you know if you're progressing toward your goal? You must find a method to quantify your success. Let's say your goal is to save up money. You can monitor how much you spend per week and see if you can meet your savings goal.

Attainable: Set a goal that can realistically be achieved. With your current resources, is it possible to attain it? If it's not possible, think about how you can acquire them.

Relevant: Is your goal important to you and your plans? Does it fit in with what you want to accomplish in life? Ensure that your goal conforms to your principles and long-term ambitions.

Timely: At what point do you aim to attain your goal? Establishing a time limit creates a feeling of immediacy and spurs you to act. Ensure that the time you set for the deadline is possible.

Step #2: Write Down Your Vision

When you have a goal, it's crucial to envisage what it will feel like when you achieve it. It implies having a precise understanding of what you wish to accomplish and the appropriate way to carry out the plan. When setting a goal, consider: who, what, when, where, and why. Don't just say "I want" or "I will." Instead, describe how you will feel once you reach your goal.

For example, you can draft something like: "Caring for our minds and emotions is imperative, especially when going through the tough times of being a teenager. I envision creating a friendly and welcoming place at my school where we can all talk about our problems, help each other, and make sure we feel good mentally. I plan to arrange events like workshops, groups to support each other, and campaigns to raise awareness. I aim to ensure everyone feels supported and that it's okay to focus on our mental health."

Step #3: Learn to Motivate Yourself

Write down the main reasons for your vision, as this will remind you of your purpose, plan, and how it applies to you. These questions will navigate you in that direction:

- How does this hold significance in your present life?
- In what way will this aid you or other people?
- Why should your future self continue to pursue this goal?

Remember that being truthful to oneself is essential as it will bring you back to your genuine intentions.

Step #4: Identify Your Guidelines

While encouraging messages can be uplifting, and a confidence boost can motivate people to pursue their goals, any plan may fizzle out like a smoldering fire without more precise directions.

Here are some ideas based on the given sample vision above:

Why should I do this?	How can I turn this into reality?
I envision creating a warm, friendly, and inclusive community where everyone feels supported and appreciated.	Research on mental health resources and programs available in our school.
I want me and my fellow students to learn how to prioritize our mental well-being, manage stress, focus on our	Talk to the school administrators or counselors and discuss how to make my ideas happen.

studies better, and engage more effectively in school activities.	
I want to break the stigma and for young people like me to feel comfortable discussing our mental health issues and seek the help we need.	Recruit students passionate about mental health and want to make a difference.
We build a stronger, more compassionate community by prioritizing mental health and supporting one another.	Create workshops and curricula about self-care and mental well-being.

Step #5: Create an Action Plan

Sometimes, the goals you set for yourself must be more specific, making it hard to get started. It is when you begin designing an action plan that breaks down each step you need to take to achieve your goals.

Feel free to provide a comprehensive explanation for clarity. Consider it from this perspective: Can someone else understand and follow your plan if you can't continue?

Take a look at this sample action plan:

ACTION PLAN
Research on mental health resources, programs, and support available in schools.
1. Check if there are any mental health initiatives already in place at school. 2. Find successful models of safe and inclusive spaces for mental health support. 3. Collaborate with school administration by scheduling a meeting to discuss my vision and seek their support. 4. Share ideas for creating a safe and inclusive space. Discuss potential collaboration opportunities, resources, and logistics.
Form a mental support team of like-minded students who share my passion for mental health.
Divide tasks and responsibilities among the team members, including arranging workshops, coordinating peer support groups, and organizing awareness campaigns.
Organize workshops and seminars.
1. Create an engaging workshop curriculum that covers

relevant subjects such as stress management, self-care, and coping strategies.
2. Invite guest speakers and mental health professionals to share their expertise and insights during the workshops.

Regularly evaluate and adjust existing programs.

1. Continuously gather feedback from participants to evaluate the effectiveness of the initiatives and make necessary adjustments.
2. Adapt and enhance existing programs based on the needs and suggestions of students to ensure their relevance and impact.
3. Work closely with the school administration to establish a sustainable and growing mental health support system.

Step #6: Set a Deadline

Having learned how to achieve your objectives, it's time to pick a deadline. Choose a deadline sooner than it would take to finish if you worked at an average pace. By doing this, you'll be motivated to work faster and avoid making excuses. Also, remember that you can set different deadlines for different parts of your action plan. More importantly, be unique and have fun with the process!

Step #7: Put the Plan Where You Can Easily See It

Keep your plan in a visible place rather than stashing it away in a drawer. Nonetheless, you don't wish for the paper to hinder your everyday tasks.

Try to find a spot where you'll see it daily, but it won't hinder you. Some people pin it on the fridge or a bulletin, but you can choose whatever works best for you. You can keep it on your study desk or a bulletin board in your bedroom. Be creative and find a unique spot that suits you!

Step #8: Share Your Plans

Remember to appreciate friends and family's help in achieving your goals. They can be valuable allies, so include them in your plans. They have valuable resources and connections that can assist you along the way.

Step #9: Track Your Progress

If your goal requires daily tasks, one way to track your progress is by marking each day on a calendar with red X marks or smiley face stickers. You should constantly monitor even if unexpected changes occur. It is normal to feel discouraged when progress seems slow, but keeping a record of your progress will motivate you daily.

Step #10: Acknowledge and Appreciate Your Accomplishment

There will be times when you perform exceptionally well, which is a reflection of your best self. It's important to acknowledge and remind yourself of the positive things you're doing and to take breaks when needed.

Nevertheless, ensure that the rewards you give yourself are consistent with your objectives. For example, if your goal is to raise $500 for books, don't spend a portion of the funds to buy something unrelated to books. Instead, purchase a book you've wanted to read for the longest time. Remember, choose rewards that are productive and align with your vision.

Step #11: Observe the 4 R's

Reviewing, reflecting, and refining your goals helps you stay focused, motivated, and accountable. It ensures your goals remain relevant and achievable while promoting personal growth and development.

- **Review**: Start by reviewing your goals regularly, such as monthly or quarterly. Look at what you've accomplished and still need to work on.

- **Reflect**: Take time to reflect on your progress and the challenges you've faced. Reflect on what went smoothly and what didn't, and the reasons behind it.

- **Refine**: Based on your review and reflection, refine your goals and action plan. Adjust timelines or strategies if they're not working, and consider new approaches if necessary.

- **Recommit**: Finally, recommit to your goals by reminding yourself why they're important to you and the impact achieving them will have on your life. Stay motivated and focused on the result, but be flexible and willing to adjust.

How to Prioritize When Everything Seems Important

It's easy to get trapped in a quagmire of tasks if you have the "Everything is Imperative" mindset. Of course, details matter, and so is finishing tasks on time.

Knowing how to prioritize your work heap benefits, including but not limited to:

- Improved focus and productivity
- Reduced stress levels and feelings of social insecurity
- Better work-life balance

So, let's drop the big question: How do you prioritize things when everything seems consequential?

Create a Task Master List

The basic among the basic— if you have goals, creating a list helps you navigate the sea of to-do's and achieve clarity in the process. Break down more significant tasks into subtasks to avoid getting overwhelmed. Once done, it's time to add supplementary information, such as:

- Level of urgency or importance
- The duration required to complete each task
- Due date

Having all your tasks listed in one place allows you to have a big-picture view of your workload, understand how much work is involved, and determine which tasks require immediate attention.

Initially, focus on gathering all your tasks in one spot without worrying about organizing them. Creating a master task list is an essential first step as it helps you organize yourself from the beginning of a project or term, making it easier to maintain organization over a more extended period.

Sample Task List

Task	Importance/ Urgency	Duration Required	Due Date
Write English Essay on Hamlet	High	3 hours	May 15
Study for Math Test	High	2 hours	May 20
Complete Science Lab Report	Medium	2.5 hours	May 25
Read Chapters 1-3 of the History Textbook	Low	1 hour	May 30
Attend After-	Low	1.5 hours	None

School Club Meetings			

Apply Task Prioritization Methods

How you organize your tasks as a student depends on your schoolwork and study habits. However, there are some task prioritization methods that you might find helpful. Here are some practical techniques for organizing your schoolwork:

Chunking Method

The Chunking Method can be a helpful tool for students like you to break down larger tasks into smaller, more manageable parts. You can apply the chunking method for tasks such as:

- Identify more significant tasks that need immediate completion, such as writing a research paper or studying for a final exam.

- Break the task down into smaller, more specific parts. For example, if you're writing a research paper, you could break it down into researching your topic, creating an outline, writing the introduction, body, and conclusion, and editing and revising.

- Set a deadline for each minor task. It will help you keep on track while staying focused as you complete each component of the more critical mission on time.

- Finish each minor task individually instead of attempting to complete the entire big task at once. It will prevent you from feeling stressed and assist you in staying concentrated.

Using the chunking method, students can break down large tasks into manageable parts, stay on track, and complete their work more efficiently.

Sample Chunking Method Application

Task	Subtasks	Due
Research for essay	Search online	May 15
	Read library books	May 17

	Take notes	May 19
Write essay	Create outline	May 20
	Write introduction	May22
	Write body paragraphs	May 25
	Write conclusion	May 27
Review and edit the essay	Edit for grammar	May 29
	Review content	May 30
	Finalize formatting	May 31

Eat the Frog Method

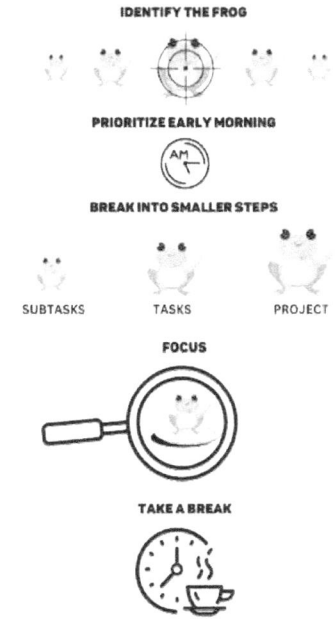

IDENTIFY THE FROG

PRIORITIZE EARLY MORNING

AM

BREAK INTO SMALLER STEPS

SUBTASKS   TASKS   PROJECT

FOCUS

TAKE A BREAK

The "Eat the Frog" method is a technique that involves tackling your most important and challenging task first thing in the morning. Starting your day doing the most demanding task makes the rest of your day easy and smooth.

It works like this:

1. Identify your most important and challenging task. Start by identifying the task you've been putting off or the one requiring the most focus and attention. It is the task that you should prioritize and complete first.

2. Begin working on the task early in the morning. Allocate some time during the early hours to focus on your top priority task. It is when you're likely to have the most energy and focus.

3. Break the task into smaller steps. If your most important task seems overwhelming, break it down into smaller, more manageable steps. Implementing this approach enables you to handle the job more efficiently and maintain motivation.

4. Stay focused. While working on your most important task, eliminate all distractions and focus solely on the current task. Avoid answering calls or texts or checking your social media account.

5. Reap benefits and rewards. Celebrate the completion of the task, such as taking a short break or rewarding yourself with a favorite snack. Doing this will make you feel competent and motivated to take on other tasks that need your attention.

Eisenhower Decision Matrix

The Eisenhower Method is a way to help you decide which tasks are most critical and which

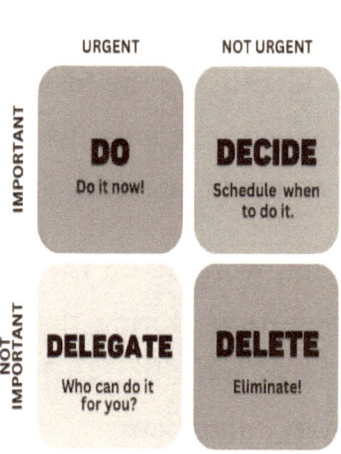

ones can wait. It involves sorting tasks into four categories based on their urgency and importance:

- Urgent and important tasks
- Important but not urgent tasks
- Urgent but not important tasks
- Not urgent and not important tasks

To use the Eisenhower Method:

1. To begin, list all the tasks that require your attention.

2. Categorize the tasks into four groups based on urgency and importance.

3. Once you have sorted your tasks, focus on completing the ones in the first two categories.

For example, a student might use the Eisenhower Method to prioritize their tasks in the following way:

- *Urgent and important tasks*: Studying for an exam tomorrow and finishing a project due later today.

- *Important but not urgent tasks*: Writing an essay due in two weeks and preparing for a presentation next week.

- *Urgent but unimportant tasks*: Responding to non-urgent emails and checking social media.

- *Not urgent and unimportant tasks*: Watching TV, playing video games.

The Eisenhower Method lets us focus on the most critical and urgent tasks first without getting distracted by less essential or non-urgent tasks.

ABCDE Method

The ABCDE method is a technique for organizing and prioritizing tasks based on their level of importance. You can label your tasks this way:

- **A- Important and Urgent:** Tasks requiring immediate attention and priority.

- **B- Important but Not Urgent:** Tasks that should be planned for and worked on immediately.

- **C- Not Important but Urgent:** Tasks that can often be delegated or delayed to focus on more critical tasks.

- **D- Not Important and Not Urgent:** Tasks that can be delayed or eliminated.

Example of ABCDE Method Application:

Level	Task	Action
A	Complete a project that is due tomorrow	Begin working on it early in the morning and reserve my entire Saturday to work on it.
A	Studying for an upcoming exam	Block off study time in my schedule and prioritize it over other tasks.

B	Attend an after-school club meeting	Attend the meeting only after completing other high-priority tasks.
C	Watch a movie with friends	Schedule it on Sunday evening only after accomplishing all high and medium-priority tasks.
D	Go shopping for new clothes	Schedule it for another weekend or after completing all high and medium-priority tasks.

E	Check your social media account	Only do this once all high and medium-priority tasks are done.

- **E- Can be Eliminated or Postponed Indefinitely:** The lowest-priority tasks; should only be done after completing all other tasks.

Use a Calendar Tool for Scheduling

A calendar is a powerful tool for managing time and scheduling tasks. For students like you, planning study time is crucial for academic success.

The following six recommendations will aid in maximizing the utilization of a calendar for studying:

- **Choose the correct type of calendar.** You have various choices that may suit your preference: paper calendars, digital calendars, or mobile apps.

- **Block out study time.** Allocate specific times for studying, and block them out in your calendar. It will remind you of your study goals, manage your time, and avoid procrastination.

- **Prioritize your tasks.** Use your calendar to prioritize your study tasks by first scheduling the most important ones. It will aid you in concentrating on the essential topics or tasks.

- **Include deadlines and exams.** Ensure you include all critical deadlines and exam dates in your calendar so you can attend them. It helps you to plan your study time and avoid cramming at the last minute.

- **Be realistic.** Don't over-schedule yourself, and leave enough time for rest, relaxation, and other activities. It helps you to avoid burnout and maintain an optimal balance between your academic and personal life.

- **Stay flexible.** Remember that unexpected events or emergencies may arise, so be prepared to adjust your schedule as needed. It helps you to stay adaptable and resilient in the face of challenges.

Organization Skills

As a student, being organized is an essential facet of your daily life. It significantly impacts on your academic performance and success.

Organization skills involve collecting information from our surroundings to perform tasks more efficiently and effectively. Often, organization skills are linked to our capability to prioritize and plan, which are also crucial executive functioning skills.

So, what are some specific skills and behaviors involved in an organization?

- Arranges items or images in a specific sequence

- Tells a coherent story with a clear beginning, middle, and end

- Uses visual aids or drawings to help return items to their proper place

- Maintains a tidy and orderly workspace, including toys and personal belongings

- Comes to school or work prepared with all necessary materials

- Creates an outline or list to organize tasks and topics systematically

If we had a minimum level of organization, it would soon be that our familiar world would fall apart. We depend on having an organized way of life, both in our homes and in our schools.

Studies demonstrate that people who possess strong organizational skills and use them efficiently experience positive outcomes in multiple areas of well-being (Indeed, 2021). Meanwhile, experts often link disorganization to higher rates of stress and distraction. Students who lack organizational skills tend to struggle more academically, receive lower grades, and have harmful interactions with teachers.

Types of Organization Skills

1. Internal Organization Skills

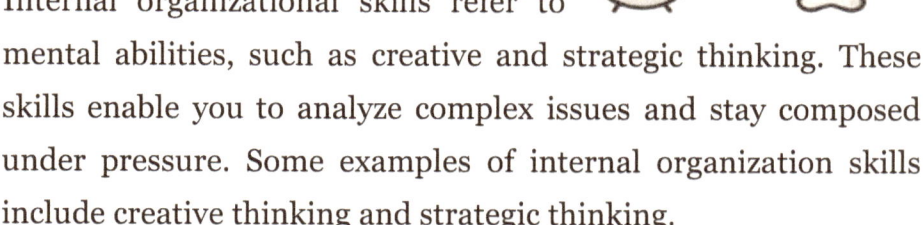

Internal organizational skills refer to mental abilities, such as creative and strategic thinking. These skills enable you to analyze complex issues and stay composed under pressure. Some examples of internal organization skills include creative thinking and strategic thinking.

Example: You use a creative visual storyboard to present a project or provide a solution to a particular problem.

2. External Organization Skills

External organizational skills involve working with others, keeping the workspace tidy, setting timelines, breaking down goals, communicating, and collaborating. These skills enable effective teamwork, including prioritization, documentation, workflow management, and collaboration.

Good external organizational skills are essential for playing well as a team member.

Example: A group of students collaboratively prioritize their tasks, document their progress, and manage their workflow effectively to complete a group project.

Essential Organization Skills for You

Below are the critical organization skills and how they can improve your growth as a student and professional later on:

Organization Skills	Description

Spatial Organization	It is the skill of arranging physical spaces to increase efficiency and reduce clutter. **Example**: Organizing study materials in labeled folders or binders.
Strategic Thinking	It is a problem-solving ability that involves analyzing situations to develop practical solutions for an organization. **Example**: Developing a study plan for an upcoming exam.
Time Management	The ability involves the capacity to prioritize tasks appropriately.

	Example: Creating a study schedule to allocate time for different subjects.
Note-Taking	It is the skill of capturing important information from lectures, readings, or discussions. **Example**: Using abbreviations and symbols to jot down essential points quickly.
Effective Communication	It is the skill of sharing thoughts, ideas, and knowledge in a manner that the receiver can comprehend. It includes speaking or writing clearly to ensure clarity. **Example**: Conveying

	ideas, collaborating with teammates, and using appropriate tone and body language to prevent misunderstandings during a group project.
Memory Techniques	The use of mnemonic devices or memory aids to help recall information. **Example**: Using the acronym "ROYGBIV" to remember the colors of the rainbow.
Goal-Setting	It is breaking down a larger goal into smaller, achievable steps with deadlines, which allows you to stay focused and motivated to achieve the desired outcome.

	Example: When preparing for final exams, you break down topics and assign a schedule so that you can cover all materials before the big day.
Task Initiation	The ability to start a task and maintain focus until completion. **Example**: Start with the most challenging task on the to-do list to avoid procrastination.
Self-Monitoring	The skill of tracking progress and adjusting strategies as needed. **Example**: Evaluating study habits regularly and making adjustments to

	improve efficiency.

Time Management

Time management is organizing and managing your time effectively to prioritize important tasks. You can accomplish more as a result.

What Advantages Does Time Management Offer?

Reduced Stress: Effective time management allows you to avoid the stress of constantly feeling overwhelmed and having too much to do. You can accomplish your goals without feeling rushed or stressed by planning tasks and managing your time well.

Life Balance: Good time management skills allow you to balance your academic and personal life. With a well-organized schedule, you can allocate sufficient time to study, work, and other activities, while still having time for relaxation and socializing.

More Freedom: Effective time management gives you more control over your life. You can plan your time to accommodate their priorities and interests and enjoy more freedom to pursue your goals without feeling constrained.

Greater Focus: Time management helps you focus and concentrate on a specific task and avoid distractions that can derail your progress. You can allocate specific times for different activities by scheduling your time, enabling you to stay on track and focused.

High Productivity Level: Good time management increases productivity since you can complete your work on time without sacrificing quality. This also allows you to accomplish more quickly and achieve your academic and personal goals.

Less Procrastination: You can avoid procrastination, which can be a significant obstacle to success. With a well-organized schedule, you can plan your work and stay motivated to complete your tasks on time.

Less Distraction: Good time management can help you avoid distractions that can interfere with your productivity and success.

By scheduling and prioritizing your time, you can concentrate on crucial tasks and prevent disruptions that impede your progress.

Increased Energy: To improve your energy levels, you can plan your tasks and activities for when you are the most attentive and concentrated. It helps you avoid burnout and fatigue while staying energized and productive throughout the day.

More Time to Think: You can allocate time for reflection and contemplation essential for personal growth and development. Giving time for self-reflection and innovative thinking enables you to acquire fresh viewpoints and ideas to accomplish your objectives.

How to Practice and Develop Time Management Skills

1. Set clear goals: Define your short-term and long-term goals to provide direction and purpose for your time management efforts.

2. Prioritize tasks: Identify the most critical and urgent tasks that must be done first. Use techniques like the Eisenhower Matrix (categorizing tasks into four quadrants: urgent and important, important but not urgent, urgent

but not necessary, and neither urgent nor essential) to prioritize effectively.

3. Create a schedule: Develop a daily, weekly, or monthly plan that allocates specific time blocks for activities, including work, study, breaks, and personal commitments. Use digital or physical planners, calendars, or time-management apps to organize your schedule.

4. Break tasks into smaller steps: To avoid getting overwhelmed, break down large tasks into smaller chunks for them to be manageable. It makes these tasks easier to focus on and prevents you from procrastination.

5. Eliminate distractions: Minimize distractions that steal your time and attention. Go to a place where you can be peaceful and comfortable. Turn off social media, and use website blockers or apps that limit your access to time-wasting websites or apps.

6. Practice the Pomodoro Technique: This involves working on a task for a focused period, typically 25 minutes, and a 5-minute break. After completing four cycles, take a longer break of 15-30 minutes. This method helps maintain focus and productivity.

7. Learn to say "no": Don't overcommit yourself. Don't say yes when you don't want to do it. Spend your time and energy only on things that truly matter.

8. Delegate and outsource: Delegate tasks to others or outsource specific responsibilities. It lets you concentrate on more important tasks or activities that align with your goals.

9. Review and adjust: Regularly evaluate your time management practices. Assess what's working and what's not, and make necessary adjustments to improve your efficiency and productivity.

10. Take care of yourself: Proper time management includes self-care. Ensure you allocate time for rest,relaxation, exercise, and activities you enjoy. Self-care enhances productivity and effectiveness.

Remember, developing time management skills is an ongoing process. Be patient with yourself and remain committed to practicing these techniques consistently.

Is Multitasking Effective?

Simultaneously juggling multiple tasks is not productive for students because it can result in reduced efficiency, heightened stress, and inferior work quality. Focusing on a single task and accomplishing it before starting the next one is a superior method for achieving peak learning and performance.

Drawbacks of Multitasking and Its Effects on Your Mental Health

Multitasking has become a common practice even among students. However, it is detrimental if one considers productivity. Instead, it can cause more harm than good to mental health and overall performance. Here's how they can negatively affect your mental well-being:

It increases your stress levels. Multitasking can spike stress levels as you constantly switch between tasks, creating an overwhelming feeling and contributing to anxiety and difficulty managing workloads effectively.

It reduces your productivity. Decreased productivity: Contrary to popular belief, multitasking often reduces efficiency and productivity, dividing your attention and making it difficult to concentrate on tasks fully.

A study has shown that multitasking can reduce productivity by 40% (*Multitasking: Switching Costs*, 2006). This only means that you will need help tackling your tasks efficiently. Impaired focus and concentration: Constantly switching between tasks can hinder your ability to focus and concentrate.

It also limits your ability to think deeply and engage in creative problem-solving, hindering innovative thinking and affecting your ability to generate new ideas.

It decreases your focus and concentration. Multitasking requires constant attention-switching, which can reduce your ability to focus and concentrate on individual tasks. It may lead to decreased accuracy, more mistakes, and reduced overall performance.

It impacts memory retention. Multitasking can lead to information overload and make it harder for your brain to retain information, leading to forgetfulness and decreased memory retention.

You are most likely to commit mistakes. Pay attention to essential details, as you can only partially focus on each task.

It affects your overall mental health. Juggling tasks will only leave you anxious, frustrated, and overwhelmed. Multitasking demands more mental effort and can exhaust your cognitive resources. It can leave you feeling mentally drained, tired, and unable to perform at your best. Of course, this will negatively impact your mental well-being over time.

To promote better health, it is generally advisable to do one task at a time, prioritize essential activities, and incorporate breaks to rest and recharge.

Things to Do Instead of Multitasking

You can utilize various productivity techniques instead of multitasking, such as the ones below:

Prioritize your tasks. Create a list of your duties and prioritize them in order of importance. Use techniques such as the Eat the Frog, ABCDE method, etc.

Example: Make a to-do list and rank them according to importance or urgency.

Use time-blocking. Dedicate time slots in your schedule to work on certain tasks. During these times, eliminate all distractions and focus solely on the current assignment.

Example: Schedule specific blocks of time for each task on your to-do list, and work on only one task during each designated time block.

Implement batch-processing. Create clusters of related tasks and accomplish them in a single session. This method can boost efficiency and help maintain focus on one type of assignment at a time.

Example: Dedicate a specific day of the week to complete all assignments and another day to study for exams.

Take breaks. Instead of trying to work on multiple tasks simultaneously, take breaks in between tasks to refresh your mind and improve your productivity.

Example: Take short breaks throughout the day to recharge and refocus, such as walking, stretching, or meditating.

All the methods mentioned above are essential to overall general management. Applying the different strategies can help to improve your performance and management skills to ensure success in the future.

Developing and strengthening executive functioning skills can lead to improved self-control, enhanced problem-solving abilities, better decision-making, and increased overall success in various domains of life. Now that you have learned about it, the next chapter will discuss healthy eating habits and budgeting.

CHAPTER 3

Savvy Eats: Nourishing Your Body, Saving Your Wallet

"Healthy eating doesn't have to break the bank. It's about making smart choices and getting creative with your resources. Nourishing your body with wholesome, affordable foods is an investment in your long-term well-being."

M aintaining a healthy lifestyle is often associated with high costs and expensive grocery bills in today's fast-paced world. However, this perception needs to be debunked. In reality, nourishing your body with wholesome, nutritious foods doesn't have to drain your wallet. It's all about making intelligent choices and getting creative with the resources available to you.

You need to learn these skills to prepare yourself for college life later. Living away from a budget and from your parents will be challenging. You will do everything by yourself, including budgeting, grocery shopping, cooking, and, most importantly, healthy eating to keep yourself physically fit and mentally healthy to cope with everyday challenges.

Healthy eating is not just a short-term trend or a temporary fix; it's a long-term investment in your well-being. You take proactive steps toward a healthier and happier future by prioritizing nutritious foods.

You don't need to splurge on expensive superfoods or exotic ingredients to achieve optimal health. Instead, the key lies in understanding the nutritional value of everyday foods and making informed choices.

One of the fundamental principles of eating healthily on a budget is to focus on whole, unprocessed foods. These foods provide essential nutrients, vitamins, and minerals for a balanced diet. Incorporating them into your meals allows you to optimize your health without spending a fortune.

Getting creative with your resources is another vital aspect of affordable, healthy eating. It means utilizing leftovers, meal planning, and innovative ways to repurpose ingredients. Furthermore, adopting a mindful approach to shopping can significantly impact your finances and overall health.

Ultimately, healthy eating is not a luxury reserved for the privileged few. It's a lifestyle choice that everyone can embrace, regardless of financial circumstances. By making intelligent choices, prioritizing whole foods, and getting creative with your resources, you can nourish your body, boost your well-being, and set the stage for a healthier future. Remember, investing in long-term health is a priceless gift yielding immeasurable benefits for years.

Smart Groceries Shopping

Regarding grocery shopping, finding a balance between nourishing your body and being conscious of your spending is essential. By planning and using your imagination, you can optimize your budget without compromising the food quality you bring home. Purchasing groceries on a limited budget requires adopting clever shopping strategies, making thoughtful decisions, and being open to exploring alternative options. You can prepare delicious and wholesome meals while managing your expenses by prioritizing affordable and nutritious ingredients. Embark on this journey of budget-friendly grocery shopping, making deliberate choices that benefit your health and finances. With careful planning and resourcefulness, you can enjoy nutritious meals without exceeding your budget and achieve your health goals while remaining mindful of your financial well-being.

How to Buy Grocery on a Budget

A few like to do it, and others hate it — we're discussing grocery shopping. Meal budgeting for you or your entire family can make anyone's head spin. However, who says grocery shopping must be tricky while on a budget?

The best information is that you can save your entire budget for delicious food. With a few advanced making plans and creativity, you could eat balanced, healthy meals that your whole family loves.

You may reduce your monthly grocery spend, stay within your budget, and reach your financial objectives more quickly by forming a few new habits. That means you'll have more money toward debt repayment, future investments, or fun purchases like a lovely meal out where the cooking and clean-up are taken care of!

Try one of these money-saving tips on your next trip to the grocery shop. The money that stays in your pocket may surprise you. You might also develop a lot more culinary creativity.

Explore your Pantry

Look through your refrigerator or pantry to see what meals you can assemble with your current ingredients. When you have some perfect chicken thighs stuffed in your freezer and cans of cream and pineapple chunks, who says you need to stock up on more groceries? You already have saved a lot of money using the food, even if you still need to buy a few things.

Consider Your Options

Bulk purchasing is fantastic when you do indeed save money. However, it is not always true that buying in bulk from a discount store will save you money. Be mindful of comparing the price per unit or ounce for the item you're buying when grocery shopping on a tight budget.

Only buy items you need, especially when it comes to perishable things, despite how alluring it may be to store up. Buying bulk cereal is a wise investment for a family of four or more. But if you're alone, you should pass on the 40-count container of Greek yogurt.

Know When to Replenish Your Stock

Good timing is crucial in getting a good deal. According to several experts, buying food on Wednesdays is more affordable. That's because grocery retailers refresh their shelves mid-week and mark down items that weren't popular the previous week. However, they'll occasionally give you the price reductions from last week's sale because they're adjusting the discounts. Try to avoid the weekends if going on a Wednesday is not feasible. Fewer deals result from larger crowds.

Deals are greatly influenced by the time of day as well. Early birds get the first go at the discount racks! Shopping just before closing time, when the deli and bakery counters are attempting to sell off the remainder of their stock, is another excellent opportunity to earn significant discounts if you're a slow shopper.

Plan and Stick to Your Grocery List

Make your grocery lists before shopping. It saves you from impulsive buying, which may lead to the fast depletion of your food budget. When planning to reduce your grocery bill, this is an excellent way to do it. Before you leave the house, make a grocery list and a meal plan. Follow the list when you go to the store. Don't leave allowance for unexpected expenses that go over budget. Allow your children to assist in meal planning and item discovery while you shop as a family (it's like a scavenger hunt in the grocery store!). Staying within your budget is much simpler when you shop strategically and collaborate.

Call for Curbside Collection

Order your groceries for curbside pickup to avoid buying on impulse. When you can enter all the information you require in a search bar, resisting temptations is much simpler.

Online shopping makes it simple to compare brand prices, check what's on offer, and see the total come up without a calculator in real time! No more standing in line to pay to find that the family-size cereal box is not on sale.

Another benefit of grocery delivery? Avoiding the store will ultimately save you a ton of time and money. Remember that saving time means saving money. While some grocery stores provide free curbside pickup, others levy a nominal cost. Just be sure to factor any additional costs into your budget.

Buy Fresh Fruits and Vegetables in Season

Following this guideline when grocery shopping on a tight budget is crucial. Avoid buying expensive pomegranates in mid-July and choose seasonal fruits and veggies instead. This way you will get the freshest and tastiest produce while also saving money.

Print out a helpful listing of products and stick it to your refrigerator. This way, you'll constantly know what goods are in season while heading to the grocery store. Buying domestically grown produce helps stimulate your community's economy, and freshness is always guaranteed.

Avoid Eye-Level Objects

Have you ever observed that the priciest things on the grocery store shelves are situated directly above your line of sight? That is not by chance. Food markets are wise. They want you to look at those things and spend money.

Instead of falling for those marketing ploys, scan the store from top to bottom. The less expensive brands are frequently found higher or lower on the shelves. Consider it a treasure hunt to find the best deal.

Keep Non-Perishable Goods Online

Merchandise like protein bars and dried fruits are perfect for purchase from online shops like Amazon. It saves you cash because you won't have to pay food tax; if delivery is free, that's an added incentive. Just make sure to check the products' expiration dates.

Re-Evaluate Dinner

Give yourself a break and relax if the term "dinner" conjures up images of a substantial home-cooked meal featuring a fine piece of meat, two steaming sides of fresh vegetables from the farmers market, warm French bread, and a chocolate dessert. It's not 1952; supper doesn't need to be a lavish spread. BLTs, beans, omelets, or you eat a sizable meal a few times weekly.

Feel free to serve straightforward meals or breakfast for dinner to stretch your grocery budget. Utilize the fact that children enjoy eating pancakes for dinner. Eggs are inexpensive, and if you're feeling fancy, you can make them into various dishes like frittatas and quiches. Or, keep things straightforward with some egg salad sandwiches.

Your guilt and grocery bill can decrease with a creative rearranging of the evening meal. Additionally, you'll save a ton of time by forgoing the daily preparation of a three-course dinner. Freedom!

Do Your Calculation

You'll avoid any unpleasant surprises at the checkout counter if you keep an ongoing count of the amount of money in your cart. Get your phone calculator open and keep track of all the items you're adding to your cart. It may cause you to pause and consider if you require the pricey $5 sparkling water that isn't on sale.

Round up Digits

When you run out of ideas to cut grocery costs, try this amusing little prank on yourself. With your calculator in hand, round the price of each item as you move around. You get the picture. The $1.49 item becomes $2, and the $7.75 item becomes $8. If you follow these steps for every item in your basket, you'll still have a general idea of how much you're spending, but you'll be pleasantly pleased to always come in under budget when you're at the checkout counter.

Start Storing and Freezing Meals

Come up with a food budget. Online, there are a ton of recipes for freezer meals. Find them out! You can set aside a Saturday to prepare many freezer meals, then benefit from them later. By saving money, you'll also save time. Plus, you don't need to have the same dinner every day because You worry that your supplies may spoil.

Use Cash to Pay

Cash is king, as we like to say around here! Sticking to your shopping budget and paying with cash are the most remarkable ways to guarantee that your final total will be cheaper. When you have cash on hand and head to the store, you know how much you can spend because once it is gone, it's gone.

Additionally, it will assist you in prioritizing meat and veggies over ice cream and cookie impulse purchases. Those minor additions are acceptable, but you must prepare for them.

Take out cash for groceries every week rather than once a month if you discover that you are dining like royalty at the beginning of the month but barely get by at the end.

Try Hopping at Various Grocery Stores

Why did you decide to shop at the current supermarket? Is it the most welcoming? Is it along your commute or the one closest to your house? If we're open, shop where we do just out of habit.

It might be time to stop patronizing your favorite grocery store; we know it isn't effortless. The least expensive grocery stores like

Walmart, Trader Joe's, and many others exist. But bear in mind that things may differ locally, so if you need clarification on which grocery stores are worthwhile investing your time and money in, ask about and compare costs.

Sometimes, saving money on food means looking at the weekly advertising in your neighborhood to see what grocery stores around are offering on sale. In the long run, purchasing from the nearby store is more expensive.

Discover the Sales Cycles

Are you prepared to conduct some investigation? Start keeping track of when and how much your favorite things are discounted. Consider keeping a journal or using your smartphone to take note of sales trends. You'll soon be able to predict upcoming sales with ease.

Bring Your Grocery Bag

When shopping for groceries, bring your bag. If you bring in a reusable bag, many retailers will give you a discount on your entire shopping bill. How simple was that? Typically, your savings per bag range from 5 to 10 cents. Your savings from five bags could range from 25 to 50 cents. Keep a few in your car to ensure you remember your reusable bags at home.

Purchase Only What You Need

Finding forgotten fruits and veggies in the back of your refrigerator is frustrating. Realizing they're now sour or mushy is even worse because it's wasted money. It's a painful experience.

Make every effort to put what you purchase at the grocery store to good use. To assist you in remembering, post a list of your refrigerator's food inventory on the door. Don't let the food go to waste, no matter what you do.

Purchase perishable meals in portions that you'll use right away. Spoiled food about to be tossed into the rubbish is not a bargain. Shop for fresh produce in small quantities that can be consumed within a week. For instance, it's good to split up bananas or grapes in keeping with the number you want. Rather than purchasing sizable fresh produce, search for frozen fruits and greens that are less perishable. You can make healthy snacks and meals from them, so you won't have an excuse not to load up fruits and veggies.

Sales and discounts can be tempting, but it's important to consider whether you really need the items before making a purchase. Simply buying something because it's on sale could end up costing you more money than planned. Stick to your grocery list to avoid overspending, regardless of any deals available.

Forgo 'Buy one, get one' offers as well. Either you'll buy ingredients you cannot consume at all, or you'll pay an inflated price for the 'purchased' object to cover the cost of the free one.

Clip coupons with a warning. Collecting and using coupons can feel like an accomplishment. Conversely, coupons may additionally convince you to purchase objects not worth buying.

Give Your Green Thumb a Try

Why not try gardening? You may have a green thumb and save much on your veggies. You won't need to purchase tomatoes, bell peppers, or cauliflower from the supermarket if you cultivate them in your garden. Like Little House on the Prairie, walk outside and take them from your garden.

Have a yard but no garden? No issue! There are many kits available for indoor gardens. Start modestly by cultivating parsley, cilantro, and rosemary on the kitchen windowsill. Puree your produce and freeze it in ice cube trays if you can't use it now. How fantastic is that?

Utilize Apps on Your Phone

Pay attention to the numerous rebate applications available while seeking ways to reduce your grocery bill.

Some fantastic apps that can help you save money include Ibotta, Receipt Hog, Checkout 51, and Fetch Rewards. Although rebates don't offer you a discount immediately (unlike a regular coupon), you should save money over time.

Using coupons you get hold of for your Sunday newspaper seems like a thing of the past. However, thanks to apps like Ibotta and Rakuten, consumers can get hold of rebates or cashback on their grocery purchases.

Ibotta and Rakuten offer rebates on grocery objects bought from nationwide chains like Walmart and Target. You may get a hold of refunds on items purchased in-shop or online so you can use them while shopping.

Moncel and Chase both advocate the Flipp App, which lets clients go into their place and discover coupons and sales for nearby grocery shops.

Only Purchase Meat When on Sale

When it's not Meatless Monday, reintroduce meat into your diet by learning to buy it wisely. Be on the lookout for excellent meat bulk discounts. Additionally, look for beef cuts that are less expensive than the ones you often purchase. Choose chicken thighs rather than chicken breasts. Instead of sirloin, choose ground chuck. Instead of eating pork chops, pig out on pork loin.

Use Your Creativity With Leftovers

The possibilities are endless regarding using your creativity in dealing with leftovers. Create soups, casseroles, new dishes, and your leftovers to avoid tossing out what's left of your food. You can always search the internet for leftover food recipes.

Everyone is aware that eating out for lunch will significantly increase your food budget. If you spend $10 twice a week on eating out, you're paying $80 a month (and we haven't even discussed a wonderful Friday night dinner with pals). Spend less when you can use recycled leftovers and save a ton of money!

Order Generic Items

Even though you know that generic pasta is less expensive, you are still determining if it will suit your grandmother's lasagna recipe. Are off-brand products really any worse than notable brands?

According to Consumer Reports, most store brands are as tasty and high-quality as name brands, yet they're often 20–25% less expensive (*Store-Brand Vs. Name-Brand Taste-Off - Consumer*

Reports, n.d.). We experimented with a few recipes and did some arithmetic to figure out how much money you can save by buying generic foods. Just for meals, it adds up to roughly $528 a year! In other words, if you can cook as well as Grandma, which we can't help you with, your less expensive lasagna will taste just as wonderful as Grandma's. Are you not convinced? Get this: Many chefs also purchase generic versions of everyday items like salt, sugar, and baking soda.

Shop at the Farmers Market in the Evening

Okay, only some things at a farmers market will be less expensive. However, most farmers want to avoid bringing their harvest home with them at the end of the day. So explore the farmers market afterward to see what bargains you may find. Offer a fair price for the remaining box of fruit. You'll find some excellent fresh produce at a great price.

Request a Bargain

The first rule of getting a great deal is to bargain on everything, including at the grocery store. The sticker price is not the total cost but the beginning point. Everything is a bargain. All you have to do is ask. However, request a discount if the yogurt you're about to purchase has only two days left before it goes bad.

Maintain and Hide Away

Purchase ingredients in excess and can them for the winter when they overflow at the farmers market (or in your garden). In the winter, you can grab a jar of your homemade "summer in a jar" tomato sauce off the shelf and spend a few dollars on a package of pasta. When you combine everything, you have a dinner that is quite affordable. Additionally, consider how satisfying consuming the sauce you produce will be. Grandma would be thrilled with you!

And speaking of sauce, buying a vacuum sealer will help you save time and work. Plan a day when you'll prepare large quantities of flavorings, such as cheese, tomato, or curry. When you want the comfort of a tasty sauce with no effort, vacuum seal and freeze them. You only need some simmering water or a slow cooker to revitalize the sauce. Good appetite!

Shop the Store's Outside Aisles

Most of the food in the grocery store's interior aisles is processed, which can ruin your budget (and, let's face it, your diet). Locate fresh fruits, vegetables, grains, and beans in the store's periphery. You'll eventually be grateful for your food budget.

Leave the Packaging Out

A head of lettuce with some straightforward homemade dressing will cost half as much as a pre-packaged bag with a dressing packet and trimmings. Wherever possible, choose fruits and vegetables that are not packed. They are typically healthier and less expensive. Yes, chopping and preparing will take longer, but you'll finish with more money.

Search for Outlet Shops Selling Day-Old Bakeries

Buying products from those outlet stores will help you stick with your grocery budget.

Prices are reduced by way of extra than 50% from bakeries compared to supermarkets. Bread products freeze well and are flexible. You can use them in sandwiches, as well as in recipes calling for breadcrumbs and stuffing.

Beware of Shrinkflation

Food corporations have some methods of coping with rising expenses. One tried-and-authentic tactic is "shrinkflation," where the business enterprise makes the packaging smaller while retaining the same price. At the Reddit thread r/shrinkflation, lawsuits regarding shrinking maple syrup jugs and cereal packing containers started. In truth, Tillamook introduced that it might reduce the dimensions of its ice cream carton without changing the fee.

Because most customers know the item cost and now the price is different from weight, you are spending more on meals while getting less without even noticing.

When shopping, pay attention to the price per pound listed on store labels is essential so you don't mistakenly assume bigger items are always cheaper.

Blogger Erin Chase from 5 Dollar Dinners advises customers to be aware of advertising tactics used to sell products, such as placing expensive items at eye level. To avoid overspending, take the time to compare prices before adding items to your cart instead of impulsively buying the first thing you see.

Use a Grocery Rewards Card

Using the right rewards card while purchasing could save a lot of cash while buying groceries. Many credit cards have better rewards for groceries. An example is the Blue Cash Preferred, which offers cardholders 6% cash back at U.S. supermarkets on as much as $6,000 in keeping with 12 months of purchases. There's a zero introductory annual price for the first 12 months, then $95.

Never Shop When You're Hungry

Lastly, never grocery shop on an empty stomach; you will most likely buy what you don't need. When you are hungry, your decision-making is affected; buying food because you crave it is not a good decision.

People often act absurdly when they are hungry. They act like zombies while aimlessly wandering the grocery store's aisles, saying things they don't mean, and devouring their roommate's chips.

Furthermore, even though your best buddy would not hold you accountable for what you said while famished, your grocery bill will only let you off the hook if you do it. Put that bakery-bought pineapple upside-down cake back and leave the 48-count frozen waffles alone.

How to Make Grocery Shopping Healthy

Making grocery shopping healthy is essential for maintaining a nutritious diet. You can improve your overall well-being by choosing the right foods and making informed choices. This guide will provide tips and strategies to make your grocery shopping trips healthier and more beneficial for your health.

Tips on How to Make Grocery Shopping Healthier

Plan, plan, and plan. Grocery stores are displayed to encourage human beings to spend more rapidly — from the seasonal items you happen to see when you purchase the cheap chocolate bars and chips lining the checkout aisles. To avoid impulsive buying, you should plan what you need to cook that week and what you need to shop for. Pick out one or two recipes you will be making that week and place them on your agenda so you can stick to your food budget plan.

Bring your list of items to purchase before heading to the grocery store. When you have a meal plan in mind, you're less likely to wander around aimlessly thinking about what to shop for while inside the grocery store.

Avoid buying food on the go. Food on the go, such as fast food like hamburgers and French fries, is often more expensive and less healthy. These types of food contain high- fat levels, which can be harmful to your body.

Purchase less meat. There has been a price hike of beef, chicken, and eggs, which has risen by almost 16% from August 2019 to August 2021. Rising meat costs resulted from many factors, including intense heat and droughts, which have killed the hay that farm animals consume, and salary increases for employees at meat processing factories.

Suppose you spend more on meat than on different food categories while purchasing groceries. In that case, buying less meat is a simple way to trim your bill. Meat is often the most luxurious component. Cutting down your meat intake can be as easy as imposing a few meatless days per week or using lesser meat for your recipes.

Use only half of the meat called for in a recipe, or use cheaper alternatives. Sub in beans, lentils, and mushrooms for floor pork. For chicken meat, sub in white beans and more vegetables.

Suppose you're reluctant about reducing your meat intake but still need to keep the money. In that case, you may find meat bargains at your neighborhood grocery stores and build your meal plan around what's on sale that week.

Keep away from portion-controlled snack packs. Not only are they extra expensive, but they also contain lots of calories.

Remember that not because it's sugar-free means the food is fat-free, and vice versa. Watch out for the labels and decide if those snack packs are well worth the splurge.

Limit your buying of ready-organized meals. Comfort is fantastic till you have to pay a higher price for it. Ready-made food might be convenient but more expensive than the ones you make. Having someone else put the meal together makes you pay a higher price. When you start remembering that while you're buying, you'll realize that organizing meals yourself is better.

Purchase meat and cereals in bulk. Make it a purpose to buy your meat and grain in bulk. Experts recommend shopping for sparkling beef loin and cutting it into low-fat loin chops for a roast, cubing it into chunks, or shopping for a chook and cutting it at home. In case you're not a meat eater, remember beans as a low-price protein supply. Purchase oatmeal in bulk in preference to character-flavored packs with added sugar and salt. Plus, they're cheaper.

Create your snacks, juices, and sweets. An easy way to bring snacks on the go is to buy a big package of your favorite snacks and a box of sandwich bags to pack them in.

Reduce consumption of convenience foods in cans and packages by shredding your lettuce and cheese (cheeses frequently freeze nicely!).

Once a month, clean out your refrigerator and cabinets. Before purchasing more, use up what you already have. Organize the drawers and cabinets you use for food storage. If you need to know what you already own or can't find what you purchased, you'll make unnecessary purchases of more of the same. If you stockpile, be aware of expiration dates and bag the food to keep it fresh for as long as possible.

Expedite mealtimes. Pre-cook or marinate large packages of meat before freezing. It is less enticing to dine out if you know you have food prepared at home.

Once a week, wash and chop up fruits and vegetables. Preparing lunch and dinner will move more quickly, and ready-to-eat healthful snacks will be available.

How to Make a Healthy Grocery List

A healthy grocery list is essential to practice portion control, balanced eating, and mindful meal preparation to maintain a healthy lifestyle. Here's how to do it.

1. Plan your meals: Start by deciding what meals you want to prepare for the week. It will help you determine the ingredients in your grocery list.

2. Add a variety of fruits and vegetables: Aim to include a colorful assortment of fresh fruits and vegetables in your list. Fruits and veggies contain essential vitamins, minerals, and fiber. Choose a mix of leafy greens, berries, citrus fruits, cruciferous vegetables, and other seasonal produce.

3. Opt for whole grains: Include whole grain products like brown rice, quinoa, whole wheat bread, and whole grain pasta. They are abundant sources of fiber and nutrients essential for sugar blood level regulation.

4. Include lean proteins: Select lean protein sources such as skinless poultry, fish, tofu, legumes, and low-fat dairy products. These are important for building and repairing tissues and provide essential amino acids.

5. Choose healthy fats: Include sources of healthy fats in your list, such as avocados, nuts, seeds, and olive oil. Fats from these foods are beneficial for heart health and provide essential nutrients.

6. Remember dairy alternatives: If you're lactose intolerant or prefer non-dairy options, include plant-based milk, yogurt, and cheese from soy, almond, or oat.

7. Limit processed foods: Minimize processed and packaged foods high in added sugars, unhealthy fats, and sodium. Instead, focus on whole, unprocessed foods.

8. Think of your dietary needs: If you have specific nutritional requirements or restrictions, such as gluten-free, vegan, or low-sodium, include suitable alternatives.

9. Include healthy snacks: Add nutritious snacks like fresh fruits, raw nuts, seeds, yogurt, or hummus to your grocery list to avoid unhealthy snacking options.

10. Read labels: When selecting packaged foods, read the nutrition labels to understand the ingredients and make informed choices. Look for items with minimal additives and recognizable ingredients.

Creating a grocery shopping list can be beneficial for several reasons. Here are some reasons why people should make a grocery shopping list:

Saves time and money: Bringing a grocery list when shopping for food ingredients can help you save time and money. By creating a list, you can avoid wandering in the store and picking up items you don't need. You will also ensure you spend on necessary things.

Helps plan meals: A grocery shopping list can help you plan your weekly meals. Always plan your meals, list the ingredients you need, and avoid last-minute trips to the grocery store.

Reduces food waste: Making a grocery shopping list can also help reduce wasting food. When you plan your meals and only buy what you need, you can avoid buying food you don't need.

Helps with dietary restrictions: If you have dietary restrictions or allergies, creating a grocery shopping list can help ensure you only purchase items that meet your nutritional needs.

Improves nutrition: Creating a grocery shopping list can help you make healthier food choices. By planning your meals, you can ensure that you purchase various nutritious foods and avoid unhealthy impulse purchases.

A grocery shopping list can help minimize expenses in several ways:

1. Prevents impulse purchases: When you go grocery shopping with a list, you can avoid impulsive purchases of items you don't need or that are outside your budget.

2. Helps you compare prices: With a shopping list, you can compare prices and help you find the best deals to save money.

3. Reduces trips to the store: When you have a grocery list, you can have everything you need for the week, reducing the need for multiple trips to the store. It will save transportation costs, effort, and time.

A grocery shopping list is helpful in many situations, including:

- Regular grocery shopping: When you need to restock your pantry, fridge, and freezer with your typical staple foods and ingredients.

- Meal planning: When you plan your meals for the week or the month, a grocery list ensures that you have all the necessary ingredients to make your meals.

- Special occasions: When hosting a party, a holiday dinner, or a family gathering, a grocery list can help you plan and buy specific items you need.

- Shopping for specific diets: If you follow a detailed dietary plan, such as vegetarian, vegan, or gluten-free, a grocery list can help you identify the foods you need to buy to meet your nutritional requirements.

- Shopping on a budget: You can save money on your grocery bills with a grocery list to guide you to stay within the budget and keep track of what you buy.

A grocery shopping list can be helpful anytime you need to shop for groceries, whether it's a regular trip to the store or a special occasion. It can reduce stress and guide you to make more intentional and mindful purchases.

Here's an example of a healthy grocery list:

- Apples
- Bananas
- Carrots
- Broccoli
- Chicken breasts
- Ground beef
- Brown rice
- Whole wheat bread
- Almond milk
- Greek yogurt
- Eggs
- Cheese
- Hummus
- Black beans

- Tomatoes
- Avocado

This list includes a variety of fruits and vegetables, protein sources, dairy products, and pantry staples. Of course, the specific items on your grocery list will depend on your personal preferences, dietary restrictions, and meal plans.

Balanced Diet

What is a Healthy-Balanced Diet

A balanced meal is essential because it gives the body the nutrients to function correctly and maintain good health. A balanced meal typically includes foods from all the major food groups in appropriate proportions, including:

1. Carbohydrates: Carbohydrates provide energy to the body and should make up most of your calorie intake. These are found in fruits, vegetables, and whole grains.

2. Proteins: Proteins are essential for building and repairing tissues, maintaining a robust immune system, and producing hormones and enzymes. Proteins are in lean meats, fish, eggs, beans, and nuts.

3. Fats: Fats are essential for energy production, insulation, and the absorption of specific vitamins. Healthy fats are those found in nuts, seeds, avocados, olive oil, and fatty fish.

4. Vitamins and minerals: You need vitamins and minerals to maintain good health and prevent chronic diseases. They are found in many foods, including lean meats, fruits, vegetables, whole grains, and dairy products.

A balanced meal provides the body with the right combination of nutrients in appropriate amounts to support good health and well-being. Eating a balanced diet can prevent chronic diseases, maintain a healthy weight, and improve overall quality of life. A balanced meal can also help regulate blood sugar levels, improve mood, and increase energy levels.

How to Maintain a Healthy Balanced Diet

To maintain a healthy balanced diet, follow these guidelines:

1. Include a variety of nutrient-rich foods: Consume whole grains, healthy fats, fruits, vegetables, and lean proteins. It ensures you get essential vitamins, minerals, fiber, and antioxidants.

2. Portion control: Be mindful of your portion sizes to avoid overeating. Use smaller plates and listen to your body's hunger and fullness cues.

3. Stay hydrated: Ensure to consume 6-8 glasses of water daily. Limit sugary beverages and opt for water, herbal tea, or unsweetened drinks instead.

4. Limit processed foods: Minimize consuming processed and packaged foods, often high in added sugars, unhealthy fats, and sodium. Opt for whole, unprocessed foods whenever possible.

5. Reduce added sugars and salt: Limit your intake of foods and drinks with high sugar and salt content. Read labels and choose low-sugar or no-added-sugar options.

6. Choose healthy cooking methods: Use cooking methods like grilling, baking, steaming, or sautéing instead of deep-frying. It helps retain nutrients and reduces unnecessary added fats.

7. Plan and prepare meals: Plan them to ensure they are balanced and nutritious. It enables you to avoid relying on unhealthy takeout or convenience foods.

8. Eat mindfully: Pay attention to your food while savoring each bite. It helps prevent overeating and promotes better digestion.

9. Listen to your body: Eat when you're hungry and stop when you're full. Respect your body's signals and avoid emotional or stress-related eating.

10. Seek professional advice if needed: Consult with a registered dietitian or healthcare professional for personalized guidance on your specific dietary needs and goals.

Super Easy and Simple Meals

Copycat Chick-a-fil Chicken Salad Sandwich

Ingredients:

- 1/4 cup chopped celery
- 1/4 cup chopped sweet pickle relish
- 2 cups of chicken breast (cooked, shredded, or diced)
- 1/4 cup mayonnaise
- 2 tablespoons honey mustard
- Salt and pepper, to taste
- Lettuce leaves
- 4 sandwich rolls or croissants

Direction:

1. Combine the cooked shredded chicken breast, sweet pickle relish, and chopped celery in a large mixing bowl.

2. Using a separate small bowl, mix the mayonnaise and honey mustard. Pour the mixture into the bowl of chicken and stir until well combined.

3. Season with salt and pepper to taste.

4. Cut the sandwich rolls or croissants in half horizontally.

5. Lay a lettuce leaf on half of each roll or croissant.

6. Spoon the chicken salad mixture over the lettuce.

7. Use the remaining half of the roll or croissant for cover.

8. Refrigerate or serve immediately.

9. Enjoy your delicious Copycat Chick-fil-A Chicken Salad Sandwich!

Turkey Ranch Wrap

Ingredients:

- 4 large flour tortillas
- 8 slices of deli turkey
- 4 pieces of cheddar cheese
- Salt and pepper to taste
- 1/2 cup diced tomatoes
- 1/2 cup shredded lettuce

Directions:

1. Lay tortillas on a clean surface.

2. Spread a tablespoon of ranch dressing onto each tortilla.

3. Place two slices of turkey and one cheddar cheese onto each tortilla.

4. Add a handful of shredded lettuce and diced tomatoes to the turkey and cheese.

5. Season with salt and pepper to taste.

6. Roll each tortilla tightly, tucking in the sides as you go.

7. Cut each wrap in half and serve.

Optional: Add ingredients like bacon, avocado, or sliced red onion for extra flavor and texture. Enjoy!

Chicken Caesar Salad

Ingredients:

- 1 lb. chicken breast, grilled and sliced
- 8 oz. pasta (penne o fusilli)
- 1 head romaine lettuce, chopped
- 1/2 cup Caesar dressing
- 1/4 cup grated Parmesan cheese
- 1/4 cup croutons
- Salt and pepper to taste

Directions:

1. Cook the pasta according to the instructions. Boil pasta al dente following package instructions, drain, and set aside.

2. Combine the cooked pasta, chopped lettuce, sliced grilled chicken, Caesar dressing, and Parmesan cheese in a large bowl. Toss everything together until well combined.

3. Season with salt and pepper to taste.

4. Top with croutons just before serving.

Ranch Cream Cheese Ham Roll Ups

Ingredients:

- 8 ounces of cream cheese, softened
- 1/2 cup Ranch dressing
- 1/2 teaspoon garlic powder
- 1/4 teaspoon onion powder
- 1/4 teaspoon dried dill
- 1/4 teaspoon dried parsley

- 1/4 teaspoon dried chives
- 1/4 teaspoon salt
- 1/4 teaspoon black pepper
- 8 slices deli ham

Directions:

1. Add softened cream cheese, Ranch dressing, garlic powder, onion powder, dried dill, parsley, black pepper, dried chives, and salt in a mixing bowl. Mix until well combined.

2. Lay the ham slices out on a flat surface.

3. Spread in each slice of ham a thin layer of the mixture.

4. dried chives,

5. Starting from one end, roll the ham slices up tightly towards the other end.

6. Wrap the rolled-up ham in plastic and keep it in the refrigerator to firm for about 30 minutes.

7. Remove the plastic wrap and slice the roll-ups into 1/2-inch rounds.

8. Serve chilled, and enjoy!

Note: You can customize this recipe by adding sliced green onions, chopped black olives, or shredded cheddar cheese to the cream cheese mixture.

Fiesta Salad

Ingredients:

- 1 can black beans, drained and rinsed
- 1 can corn, drained
- 1 red bell pepper, diced
- 1 green bell pepper, diced
- 1/2 red onion, diced
- 1 avocado, diced

- 1/4 cup chopped fresh cilantro
- 1 lime, juiced
- Salt and pepper, to taste
- Optional: tortilla chips for serving

Directions:

1. Combine the black beans, corn, diced bell peppers, and red onion in a large bowl.

2. Fold in the diced avocado gently and chopped cilantro.

3. Drizzle the lime juice over the salad and season with salt and pepper.

4. Toss all ingredients until evenly distributed.

5. Serve with tortilla chips, if desired.

Fried Rice

Ingredients:

- 3 cups cooked rice
- 2 tablespoons vegetable oil
- 1/2 cup diced onion
- 1/2 cup diced carrot
- 1/2 cup frozen peas
- 2 cloves garlic, minced
- 2 eggs, beaten
- 2 tablespoons soy sauce
- Salt and pepper, to taste

Optional: chopped scallions for garnish

Directions:

1. Cook rice following package instructions. It's best to refrigerate leftover rice overnight, as it will be drier and easier to fry.

2. Preheat a large skillet with oil on medium-high heat. Add the diced onion, carrot, and stir-fry for about two minutes or until softened.

3. Add the frozen peas and minced garlic to the skillet. Stir-fry for about a minute.

4. To create a space at the center of the skillet, slightly push the vegetables to the side of the skillet and crack two eggs. Scramble it and cook until done.

5. Mix in the cooked rice and stir until the rice is coated in the vegetable and egg mixture.

6. Pour the soy sauce and continue stirring until everything is well combined. Add salt and pepper to taste.

7. Continue cooking the rice, stirring occasionally, until it turns golden brown and crispy.

8. Remove from heat and serve hot. You can garnish with chopped scallions for some extra flavor and color. Enjoy your homemade fried rice!

Egg Sandwich

Ingredients:

- 2 slices of bread
- 2 eggs
- 1 tablespoon of butter
- Salt and pepper, to taste

Optional: cheese, bacon, avocado, tomato, lettuce, or any other toppings of your choice

Directions:

1. Toast slices of bread in a skillet over medium heat until golden brown or in a toaster.

2. Get another pan and melt the butter in it over medium heat.

3. Pour beaten eggs into the skillet and sprinkle them with salt and pepper.

4. Cook the eggs and flip to cook the other side until done

5. If using cheese, add it to the eggs. Put the lid to cover to melt the cheese.

6. Assemble the sandwich by placing the cooked eggs on one slice of toast and adding any additional toppings you desire.

7. Top with another toasted piece, and enjoy!

Optional variations:

1. Add bacon or sausage to the sandwich for a heartier breakfast option.

2. Mash some avocado onto one slice of toast and add sliced tomato and lettuce for a healthy twist.

3. You may use a bagel or croissant for a different texture and flavor.

In summary, healthy habits are essential for overall well-being. They can lead to a longer, happier life with fewer health problems and financial burdens. Next, we will focus on transforming your home into a relaxing, pleasant place to live.

CHAPTER 4

From Chaos to Serenity: Organizing and Creating a Peaceful Living Environment

---

"Cleaning and organizing is a practice, not a project." —
Meagan Francis

K eeping a clean and organized environment is not a one-time task that you complete. It requires consistent effort and dedication.

In other words, cleaning and organizing should be treated as a habit or routine rather than done only when necessary. It's not just a task to be checked off a to-do list but a way of life that requires regular attention and maintenance. By doing so, they become a habit that requires less effort and time in the long run, resulting in a cleaner, more organized, and less stressful living or working space.

How to Organize and Keep Your Home Tidy

Cleaning your house so it will look neat and organized can be a daunting task. However, with a few simple habits and strategies, it can become a manageable and even enjoyable part of your routine. Consider these tips to help you keep your house clean and organized:

Ways to Keep Your House Organized

Develop a cleaning routine: Create a schedule that works for you, whether it's a weekly or daily cleaning routine. Consistency is key to maintaining a clean and organized home.

Declutter regularly: Go through your possessions regularly and dispose of unused or no-longer-needed items. It will help to reduce clutter and make it easier to keep your home tidy.

Organize your space: Invest in storage solutions such as shelves, drawers, and baskets to help keep your space organized. Assign everything to a specific place so that you know where to put items away after use.

Clean as you go: Try to clean and tidy up as you go about your day. For example, if you finish cooking a meal, clean the kitchen immediately instead of leaving it until later.

Involve everyone: Get the whole family involved in keeping the house clean and organized. Divide the household chores among members so everyone takes responsibility.

Stay on top of laundry: If possible, do your laundry every day so it doesn't pile up and become overwhelming.

Use cleaning products effectively: Use the right cleaning products and follow instructions carefully. Remember to wear gloves and take other safety precautions when using cleaning products.

Following these tips can keep your house clean and organized, and make it a pleasant place to be.

Home Maintenance

Teenage girls can benefit from learning home-fixing skills for several reasons:

Independence: Knowing how to fix fundamental household issues empowers teenage girls to handle common problems independently, reducing their reliance on others for assistance.

Practicality: Fixing minor issues at home saves time and money by avoiding needing to call professionals for simple repairs.

Confidence: Developing home-fixing skills boosts self-confidence and problem-solving abilities, providing a sense of accomplishment and resilience.

Preparedness: Learning essential home fixing prepares teenage girls for future responsibilities as homeowners or renters, enabling them to address issues promptly and effectively.

Safety: Understanding home fixing ensures awareness of potential hazards and promptly promotes a safe living environment by addressing electrical, plumbing, or structural problems.

Life skills: Home fixing skills are valuable life skills you can use in various situations, fostering independence and adaptability in different environments.

Remember, it's always important to prioritize safety and consult professionals for complex or potentially dangerous repairs.

Here's a comprehensive home maintenance checklist that you can use as a reference:

Monthly Home Maintenance Tasks:

- Clean or replace air filters

- Clean range hood filters

- Sanitary garbage disposal and sink drains

Quarterly Home Maintenance Tasks:

- Check the roof for possible leaks or damage

- Lubricate garage door tracks and rollers

- Check and clean the dryer vent

Bi-Annual Home Maintenance Tasks:

- Clean windows and screens

- Clean and seal tile and grout

- Inspect plumbing for any leaks

- Test the water heater and check the pressure relief valve

- Inspect and clean air ducts

Annual Home Maintenance Tasks:

- Clean and seal exterior woodwork

- Test and flush the water heater

- Check for pests and call a professional to treat them if necessary

- Power wash the exterior of the house

By following this checklist, you can quickly identify any issues. If it's not within your ability to address them, you can seek adult supervision and guidance when necessary to avoid more significant problems in the future.

Home Maintenance for Fall and Winter

Fall comes, and you need home preparation for the winter months ahead. Here are some fall home maintenance tips:

Prepare your outdoor spaces: Drain and store garden hoses, shut off outdoor water faucets, and cover or store outdoor furniture.

Check your gutters and downspouts: Free your gutters and downspouts of dead twigs, leaves, and debris. It will ensure that there are no clogs and that it is directed away from your home's foundation.

Look for gaps and cracks: Check your doors and window for any damages and cracks. It can keep warm air in and cold air out or vice versa. Seal them.

Check your heating system: Have your heat pump or furnace regularly checked to ensure it is safe, working, and in good condition.

Inspect your chimney: Have it cleaned and checked by a professional to ensure it's safe for use during the winter months.

It will prepare your home for the colder months ahead and avoid potential problems.

Check smoke and carbon monoxide detectors: Have someone see how your smoke and carbon monoxide detectors work. Are they in working order? You may need replacement batteries.

Drain outdoor hoses and sprinkler systems: Remove any water from outdoor hoses and sprinkler systems to prevent freezing and bursting.

Check outdoor lighting to see if your outdoor lighting is working correctly. Replace any burnt-out bulbs. Walking in the dark at night will be tough, making outdoor lighting especially important in the winter. Doing these can help ensure that you prepare your home for the cold months and avoid costly repairs caused by winter weather.

Home Maintenance for Spring and Summer

Give your home some attention in springtime when the winter season could have damaged your home. Here are some essential spring home maintenance tasks you can consider:

Inspect the roof: Check for any damaged or missing shingles, leaks, or signs of wear and tear. Arrange for repairs if necessary.

Clean the gutters: Clear gutters and downspouts of debris and ensure they properly function to prevent water damage.

Check the exterior: Inspect the siding, windows, and doors for cracks, gaps, or damaged areas. Repair or replace as needed.

Service the HVAC system: Schedule a professional HVAC inspection and maintenance to ensure optimal performance during the summer months. Change air filters if necessary.

Clean and repair outdoor spaces:

1. Sweep and pressure wash patios, decks, and walkways.

2. Inspect for any damages and make necessary repairs.

3. Seal or stain wood surfaces if required.

Inspect and clean the chimney: Send someone to clean the chimney. Remove any debris or nests to ensure proper ventilation.

Check the plumbing: Look for leaks in faucets, pipes, or hoses. Test outdoor sprinkler systems and ensure they are working correctly.

Maintain the lawn and garden: Trim trees and shrubs, remove dead plants, and clear away any debris. Prepare the soil for planting and start your spring gardening.

Clean and organize the garage: Declutter and dispose of any unnecessary items. Sweep the floor, check the garage door for proper functioning, and lubricate hinges and rollers if needed.

Check the foundation: Inspect the foundation for cracks or signs of settling. Address any concerns with a professional if necessary.

Clean and inspect the chimney: If you have a fireplace, clean the chimney to remove soot and debris. Ensure the damper is functioning correctly.

Check outdoor lighting: Replace any burnt-out bulbs and clean the fixtures. Consider adding or updating outdoor lighting to enhance safety and aesthetics.

Test and maintain outdoor equipment: Service your lawn mower, trimmer, and other outdoor equipment. Check batteries in outdoor lights, solar-powered devices, and automatic sprinklers.

Clean and inspect windows: Clean the windows inside and out. Check for damaged or cracked glass and have these repaired or replaced.

Clean and repair your deck or patio: Pressure wash, stain, or paint your deck and repair any loose boards or cracks.

Inspect and clean your grill: Make sure it works correctly, clean it thoroughly, and check for gas leaks.

Note: Some of these tasks on the lists may be tough for girls, but you can always seek the help of an experienced adult to do the job for you. Remember, this is a general list, and your home's maintenance tasks may vary. Always prioritize safety and seek adult guidance when needed.

DIY Home Fixes

How to Change a Light Bulb

Changing a light bulb is a simple task that can be done with a few easy steps. Follow these basic steps:

1. Ensure that the power is OFF before doing anything to the light fixture by flipping the switch or turning off the circuit breaker.

2. Find the bulb that you have to replace. If it's in a lamp, unplug the lamp before changing the bulb.

3. Wait for the bulb to cool down if it was recently turned on. Protect your hands by using gloves and prevent being burnt, especially when it's still hot.

4. Gently twist the bulb counterclockwise to loosen it from its socket. If it's a bayonet mount bulb, press and turn it until it pops out.

5. Remove the old bulb to be disposed of later.

6. Get the new bulb out of its packaging and ensure it's the correct wattage and type for the fixture.

7. Insert the new bulb into the socket and gently twist it clockwise until it's securely in place. If it's a bayonet mount bulb, insert and turn until it locks in place.

8. Turn the switch ON to have the power back and test the new bulb.

9. Dispose of the old bulb properly in the trash or recycle it.

Remember always to exercise caution when handling light bulbs, scorching ones. If you need more clarification about doing this task, consider asking someone to do it for you or send for an electrician.

How to Use a Screwdriver

Using a screwdriver is a relatively simple process. Here are the steps to follow:

1. Select the appropriate screwdriver for the job. Note that screwdrivers are for varying types and sizes of screws. Screwdrivers are for different types and sizes of screws, so choose one that fits the screw head snugly.

2. Hold the screwdriver by the handle with your dominant hand.

3. Align the tip of the screwdriver into the screw head.

4. Apply downward pressure on the screwdriver while turning it clockwise to tighten the screw or counterclockwise to loosen the screw.

5. Use the screwdriver to tighten or loosen the screw until it is fully in place.

6. Choose a different screwdriver type or size if the screw is difficult to turn. But before changing the screwdriver, you may try applying more pressure.

7. Once you have finished using the screwdriver, store it safely.

Determine the right size and type of screwdriver for this job. Using the wrong one could damage the screw or the tool. Use proper hand placement and grip to avoid slipping or injuring yourself.

How to Use a Washer

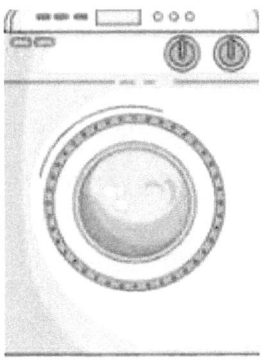

Using a washer is an essential part of home maintenance. It's important to follow these steps when using a washer. Before using a washer, you should know how it works, what types of detergent to use, and how to load it properly.

1. Choose the appropriate setting: Different washers have different settings for various types of clothing, such as delicate or heavy-duty fabrics. Choose the one suitable for your laundry.

2. Load the washer: Load your laundry into the washer. Load your washer with the required weight. Overloading it can damage the machine and affect its cleaning ability.

3. Add detergent: Add enough powder or liquid soap for the load size and type of laundry.

4. Start the washer: Close the lid and start the machine according to the manufacturer's instructions.

5. Complete the operation: Wait for the washer to complete its process before opening the lid. Once done, you can open and remove the laundry.

6. Clean the washer: After you are done with your laundry, clean the inside of the washer. You can do this by running your washer with hot water and vinegar if you don't have any specialized washer cleaner.

7. Maintain the washer: Regularly clean the washer for long-term use. Constantly check the hose and connections for leaks. Replace any parts when damaged.

Following these steps diligently can assure you of long-term use of the washer.

How to Unclog or Plunge and Drain a Toilet

Occasionally, you may experience having to deal with a clogged toilet bowl. You don't have to feel frustrated; this is a common household issue. What's essential is for you to know how to fix it. To fix a clogged toilet bow, follow these steps:

1. Stop flushing: The first step is to stop flushing the toilet. It will only cause the water to overflow and make the situation worse.

2. Remove excess water: If the water level in the toilet bowl is high, use a bucket or a cup to remove as much water as possible. It will prevent water from spilling onto the floor.

3. Plunge the toilet: Use a plunger to try to dislodge the clog. When doing this, see that the water in the bowl is enough to cover its head. Position the plunger. Push it down, and pull it up quickly to create a strong suction. Repeat this several times until the water begins to drain.

4. Use a toilet auger: If plunging doesn't work, try to use a toilet auger or a plumber's snake. Simply insert the auger into the drain and twist it to break up the clog.

5. Check the toilet trap: If neither the plunger nor using the auger works, the clog may be in the toilet trap. Remove the toilet bowl to inspect the trap for any visible blockages.

6. Call a plumber: If you can't still fix the clog on your own, try calling a plumber to avoid causing any further damage to the toilet or plumbing system.

Note: Wear gloves and use caution when fixing a clogged toilet bowl.

How to Use a Drill

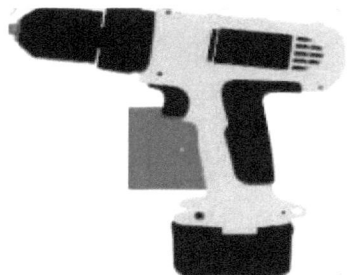

Using a drill is relatively simple, but

following safety guidelines to avoid injury is essential. Here are the basic steps:

1. Every drilling task requires a suitable drill bit. Select the drill bit size appropriate for the material you're drilling into.

2. Secure the drill bit to the drill. Test to see if the drill holds the bit in place. Drills have adjustments that allow you to tighten or loosen the chuck.

3. Adjust the drill speed. Most drills have variable speed settings, so you can adjust the speed of the drill according to the material you're drilling into. Start with a slower speed for rigid materials like metal and a faster rate for softer materials like wood.

4. Mark the spot you want to drill. Make a slight marking on the area where you want to make a hole using a pencil or marker.

5. Hold the drill steady and apply gentle pressure. Position the drill bit on the marked spot and hold the drill steady with both hands. As you start to drill, apply a slight pressure.

6. Drill the hole. Continue drilling until you've reached the desired depth. You may need to periodically release the trigger and pull the drill bit out to remove debris.

7. Turn off the drill and remove the bit. Once you've finished drilling, turn off the drill and remove the bit from the chuck.

Note: Wear safety goggles and protective gloves when using a drill. Also, read and follow the manufacturer's instructions.

How to Change Air and Water Filter

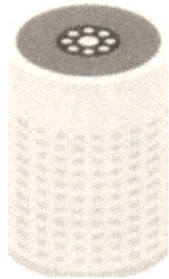

The process for changing an air or water filter can vary depending on the specific equipment or appliance involved. However, here are the usual steps you can follow when you need to change your air or water filters:

Changing an Air Filter

1. **Locate the air filter:** Typically, air filters are located behind a grate or panel on the HVAC system, furnace, or air conditioner. Refer to the owner's manual to find the air filter's location.

2. **Turn off the HVAC system:** Before removing the old filter, turn it off to prevent it from eliminating debris or dust during the replacement process.

3. **Remove the old filter:** Carefully remove the old filter from its housing. Be sure to note the airflow direction, which will be important when installing the new filter.

4. **Insert the new filter**: Take the new filter to replace the old one, matching the airflow direction. Ensure that the filter is snugly in place.

5. **Turn on the HVAC system:** After replacing the filter, turn on the HVAC system and monitor it for any unusual sounds or issues.

Changing a Water Filter

1. Locate the water filter: Depending on the appliance, the filter may be located inside a compartment or housing or attached to the water line itself. Consult the owner's manual to find the location of the filter.

2. Turn off the water supply: Before touching the filter, shut off the appliance's water supply to prevent leaks or water damage.

3. Take out the old filter: Depending on the type of filter, it may be as simple as twisting or pulling it out of its housing. You may need to remove screws or other parts to access other filters.

4. Install the new filter: Take the new filter and install it in the housing, following the instructions provided in the owner's manual. Be sure to match the flow direction.

5. Turn on the water supply: Once the new filter is in place, you can turn back the water supply. Check for any leaks or drips to ensure you did it right.

Note: Always refer to the specific instructions provided by the manufacturer for your particular equipment or appliance, as these steps may vary slightly depending on the model and type of filter.

Safety Tips for Using Handy Tools

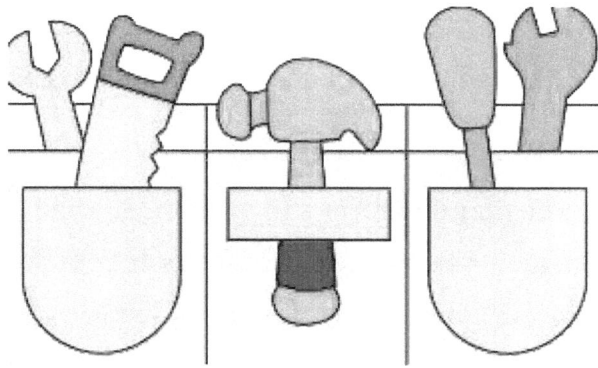

Handy tools can be a great way to tackle various tasks around the house, but using them safely is essential. Here are some safety tips for using handy tools:

1. Wear Personal Protective Equipment (PPE): Wear protective gear such as safety glasses, gloves, and ear protection to keep you safe while using the tools.

2. Keep your tools in good condition: Always inspect them before use, ensuring they are in good condition and appropriately maintained.

3. Use the right tool: Always use the right tool for the job. Using the wrong tool can make the job harder and cause accidents.

4. Keep your work area clean: Keep your workplace free from clutter. This will prevent accidents and make it easier for you to use your tools.

5. Follow the manufacturer's instructions: Read and follow the instructions provided. Handy tools come with an instructional guide. This manual will guide you on the proper use and maintenance of your tools properly.

6. Use tools in a well-lit area: Ensure your work area is well-lit, making it easier to see what you're doing and preventing accidents.

7. Keep children and pets away: For safety, keep children and pets away from the workplace to prevent them from getting injured.

8. Take breaks: Take regular breaks to prevent fatigue, which can lead to accidents.

9. Never modify your tools: Never modify them, as this can compromise their safety and make them more dangerous.

10. Store your tools properly: Store them in a secure and dry location to prevent accidents and keep them in good condition.

Knowing how to clean and maintain your home is significant to home budgeting and safety. Now that we know how it's essential to learn to turn your home into a sanctuary, the next chapter will teach you budgeting, saving, and investing in preparing you for success.

CHAPTER 5

How to Adult Like a Boss: Mastering Money Management and Career Planning

"Saving money isn't about being able to buy bigger and better things; it's about being prepared for the unexpected." "

W hile it's common to view saving money as a means to buy luxurious and desirable items, shifting our mindset and recognizing its greater purpose is essential. Saving money is not just about instant gratification. Still, it emphasizes the importance of having a long-term outlook and recognizing that financial stability and security are more valuable than temporary material possessions. Saving money is crucial to prepare for unforeseen events or emergencies, such as losing your job, medical emergencies, or major repairs. By thoughtful budgeting and shifting our perspective on saving money, we can embark on a journey of personal growth - a commitment to cultivating a strong foundation of resilience and preparedness. It's essential to remember that saving money is not just for the present but for planning a secure and stable future.

Money Management

How to Budget

Determine your income sources. Start by identifying all available income sources, such as part-time jobs, scholarships, allowances, or financial aid.

Track your expenses. Record your expenses for at least a month to understand where your money is going. Categorize your expenses into essentials (tuition, rent, food) and non-essentials (entertainment, dining out).

Set financial goals. Define your financial objectives, such as setting aside a certain monthly amount. It will help guide your budgeting decisions.

Create a budget plan. Allocate your income towards different expense categories based on their priority. Ensure that your essential expenses are covered first, and allocate a reasonable amount for non-essential spending.

Reduce non-essential expenses. You can avoid unnecessary expenses if you minimize non-essentials. For example, cook meals at home instead of eating out, find cheaper alternatives for entertainment, and avoid impulse purchases.

Consider long-term expenses. Accounts for long-term expenses like textbooks, course materials, and transportation costs for the semester. Set aside funds for these items to avoid any financial surprises.

Save money. Include a savings category in your budget to build an emergency fund or save for future goals. Even small amounts held regularly can add up over time.

Review and adjust. Review your budget regularly and monitor your expenses. Make adjustments if you overspend on specific areas to stay within the budget.

Seek student discounts and deals. Take advantage of student discounts offered by various businesses and services. You can use your money on textbooks, software, transportation, etc., by availing of these discounts and deals.

Use budgeting tools. Utilize online budgeting tools or apps to help you track your income, expenses, and savings more efficiently.

Creating a student budget requires discipline and sticking to your financial plan. However, with careful monitoring and adjustments, you can successfully manage your finances throughout your college years.

How to Balance a Checkbook

To balance a checkbook, follow these steps:

Record all transactions. Write down all deposits, withdrawals, and purchases made using your checking account in your checkbook register. Include the date, description, and amount for each transaction.

Obtain bank statements. Get your bank statements for the period you want to balance. It can be obtained online or through paper statements sent by your bank.

Compare transactions. Match the transactions in your checkbook register with those on the bank statement. Check off each transaction that appears on both.

Account for outstanding transactions. Note any transactions in your checkbook register but not on the bank statement. These may include checks that still need to clear or recent debit card purchases.

Add or subtract outstanding transactions. Adjust the balance in your checkbook register by adding or subtracting the exceptional transactions to reflect the correct balance.

Reconcile the balance. Calculate all cleared transactions on the bank statement. After accounting for outstanding transactions, compare this total to the balance in your checkbook register. The two balances should match.

Adjust for discrepancies. If the balances don't match, carefully review the bank statement and checkbook register for errors or omissions. Look for any missed or duplicated entries.

Make corrections. To make your records accurate, update your checkbook register and adjust the balance accordingly if any errors or omissions are found.

Repeat regularly. Balance your checkbook regularly, ideally every month, to ensure accurate financial records and avoid overdrafts or other economic issues.

Remember to keep all your receipts and bank statements for future reference.

How to Pay Bills, Especially College Students

Here are some steps for college students to pay their bills:

Create a budget. Determine your income and expenses to understand how much you can allocate towards bill payments.

Prioritize bills. Identify essential bills like tuition, rent, and utilities, and prioritize them over non-essential expenses.

Set up automatic payments. Many billers offer automatic deduction options from your bank account on the due date.

Use online banking. Set up online banking to conveniently manage and pay your bills. Schedule payments in advance to ensure they are paid on time.

Utilize bill payment apps. Explore mobile apps that let you pay your bills from your smartphone. Some popular apps include Mint, Prism, and BillTracker.

Consider payment plans. If you cannot pay a bill in full with your income, consider contacting the biller to inquire about options that allow you to make smaller, manageable payments over time.

Seek financial aid and scholarships. Explore scholarships, grants, and other financial aid options available to college students. These resources can help alleviate the burden of bill payments.

Communicate with billers. If you're facing financial difficulties, contact your billers to discuss possible solutions, such as extended due dates or reduced payment amounts.

Minimize non-essential expenses. Reduce discretionary spending to save money for bill payments. Cut back on unnecessary purchases and find ways to save on everyday costs.

Seek part-time employment. Consider finding a part-time job to supplement your income and cover your bills. Explore on-campus job opportunities or look for remote work options.

Staying organized, planning, and communicating with billers are crucial to ensure timely payments and managing your finances effectively.

How to Save Money

Saving money is setting aside a portion of your income for future needs or goals rather than spending it all. It involves making conscious decisions about how you use and allocate your resources. Saving money provides financial security, helps you reach your goals, and prepares you for unexpected expenses. By adopting good saving habits and minor changes to your daily routine, you can effectively manage your finances and start building a solid foundation for your future.

Here are ways to save money for any financial goal.

Start with Budgeting. Track your income and expenses to know what costs to cut.

Cut unnecessary expenses. Review your spending habits and eliminate non-essential items or services.

Meal planning. Cook at home and pack your lunch instead of eating out regularly. It will save some amount.

Use discounts and coupons. Look for deals, discounts, and coupons before purchasing to save money on food, groceries, clothing, and other items.

Automate savings. We are now in a digital economy. It's possible to set up automatic transfers for your savings account, and the bank automatically withdraws from your account and puts it into your savings account. It makes saving money a priority.

Reduce energy consumption. Save your utility bills by using energy-efficient appliances and turning off lights and electric fans when not in use.

Buy generic or store brands. Generic or store-brand products offer similar quality at a lower price than name-brand items.

Shop around for better deals: Compare prices before making a big purchase to ensure you get the best price.

Cancel unused subscriptions. Avoid subscriptions or limit to what you need.

Limit impulse buying. Before purchasing, wait 24 hours to see if it's something you need or an impulse buy.

Save on gasoline. Try carpooling or using public transportation to save on fuel and parking costs.

Sell unused items. Declutter your home and sell things you no longer need or use. You can use online platforms or organize a yard sale.

Negotiate bills. Contact your service providers (e.g., internet, cable) to negotiate lower rates or explore better deals.

DIY whenever possible. Learn basic repair and maintenance skills to fix things around your home instead of hiring professionals.

Plan for significant expenses. Save money in advance for major purchases or events, such as vacations or holiday gifts.

Saving money is gradual, so start small and be consistent with your efforts.

How to Make Money as a Teen

Even teens need money. You may not have parents to support you or your bills to care for. You can make money by exploring various opportunities, and here are ways you can try.

Part-time jobs: Look for local businesses that hire teens, like retail stores, restaurants, or movie theaters.

Babysitting or pet sitting: Offer your services to neighbors or family friends who need someone to watch their children or pets.

Online freelancing: Explore platforms that connect freelancers with clients who need services like writing, graphic design, or social media management.

Tutoring: Share your expertise in a particular subject by offering tutoring services to younger students.

Yard work or house cleaning: Offer your assistance with lawn mowing, gardening, or cleaning tasks for people in your community.

Selling crafts or handmade products: Create and sell unique items online or at local craft fairs.

Paid surveys or online tasks: Sign up for websites that pay teens to complete surveys or small online jobs.

Social media influencing: Build a following on platforms like Instagram or YouTube and collaborate with brands for sponsored content.

Car washing or detailing: Provide car cleaning services to friends, family, or neighbors.

Event assistance: Offer to help with event setup, serving food, or cleaning up after parties or gatherings.

Remember to consider any legal requirements or restrictions related to age and working hours in your area.

How to Do Banking

Regarding teen bank accounts, there are a few essential things to know. Here's a summary of the vital information:

Minimum Age Requirements

Most banks have a minimum age requirement for opening an individual bank account, typically around 18 years old. However, many banks offer specific accounts designed for teenagers, allowing them to start managing their finances at a younger age, usually around 13 to 17 years old.

Parental Consent

As a teenager, you need parental consent to open a bank account. It may involve having a parent or legal guardian co-sign the account or provide written permission.

Types of Teen Accounts

Banks often offer specialized accounts for teenagers, such as student accounts or teen checking accounts. These accounts usually have specific features tailored to young customers, such as lower fees, no minimum balance requirements, and limited access to certain banking services to promote responsible money management.

Account Restrictions

Teen bank accounts may have certain restrictions to protect young customers. These can include limits on withdrawal amounts, spending limits on debit cards, and restrictions on online and mobile banking activities.

Joint Accounts

Some banks allow teenagers to open joint accounts with a parent or guardian. It will enable parents to monitor and guide their child's financial activities while gradually granting more independence.

Financial Education

Many banks offer resources and educational materials to help teenagers learn about personal finance and develop responsible habits. These resources may include budgeting tools, savings calculators, and tips for managing money effectively.

Fees and Charges

Understanding the fees and charges associated with a teen bank account is essential. While some accounts have lower fees, reading and reviewing the terms and conditions is necessary to avoid surprising costs.

Transition to Adult Accounts

When a teenager reaches legal age, which varies depending on the jurisdiction, but usually 18 or 21 years old, they may need to transition from their teen account to a regular adult account. This process may involve updating account documentation and meeting the requirements set by the bank.

Remember that specific details and offerings may vary between banks and countries. Hence, comparing options before choosing a teen bank account is always a good idea.

How to use Credit Card Responsibly

To use credit cards responsibly, follow these tips:

- Only use what is within your budget to avoid carrying a balance and paying interest.

- Plan your expenses and allocate some of your income for credit card payments. Stick to your budget to avoid overspending.

- When you can't pay the amount due, pay at least the minimum amount required on time to avoid late fees and penalties. Then pay off the entire balance to avoid interest charges.

- Monitor your statements: Review your credit card statements regularly to identify errors or fraudulent charges. Report them to your card issuer immediately.

- Minimize the number of cards: Too many credit cards can make it difficult to manage payments and increase the risk of overspending. Consider keeping a limited number of cards.

- Maintain a low credit utilization: To maintain a good credit score, it's important to keep your credit utilization low. This means you should only use a small percentage of your available credit, ideally below 30%.

- Be cautious with cash advances: Avoid using your credit card for cash advances, as they often have high-interest rates and fees. Instead, withdraw cash from your bank, use your debit card, or withdraw money.

- Understand your card benefits and fees. Consider the terms and conditions and know their annual fees, interest rates, and rewards programs.

- Limit new applications: Applying for multiple credit cards quickly can negatively impact your credit score. Only apply for new cards when necessary.

- Build an emergency fund: Having savings can prevent relying heavily on credit cards for unexpected expenses, reducing the risk of accumulating debt.

Remember, responsible credit card use involves using credit as a tool while maintaining control over your finances and avoiding excessive debt.

Jobs Hunting for Beginner

Job hunting, especially as a beginner, can bring excitement and anxiety. As a young adult with limited professional experience, it can be difficult to demonstrate your skills and find job opportunities. These difficulties include:

- Discovering employment opportunities that match your abilities and personal values.
- Polishing your resume.
- Preparing for interviews.
- Showcasing your potential and eagerness for growth.

But do not be afraid. With proper preparation, you can easily bag your ideal job.

Writing Your Resume

A resume is a compact overview, capturing your educational achievements, work experience, and valuable skills. Employers use it to learn more about you and your qualifications for a job. When seeking employment, have a skillfully crafted resume that showcases your strengths and noteworthy achievements.

Here are some suggestions when writing your resume:

Start with a solid objective statement or summary. Clearly state your career goals and what you aim to achieve with your resume.

Highlight relevant coursework and projects. Showcase academic achievements, major coursework, research projects, or practical experiences demonstrating your skills and knowledge in your field of interest.

Include part-time jobs and internships. Mention any work experience you have gained, even if it doesn't perfectly match your desired career path. Emphasize transferable skills such as communication, teamwork, problem-solving, and time management.

Showcase extracurricular activities and leadership roles. Highlight involvement in clubs, organizations, sports teams, or volunteer work that exhibits your leadership abilities, teamwork skills, and commitment.

Focus on skills and achievements. Highlight specific skills you have acquired, such as language proficiency, computer skills, or certifications. Include any notable accomplishments, awards, or scholarships you have received.

Many teenagers don't have much job experience. If you're having the same dilemma, you can use these instead:

Education: Provide a list of classes, extracurricular activities, student memberships, studies, and other relevant details related to your education.

Hobbies and Interests: Include activities that demonstrate your relevant skills and interests in this section.

Volunteering: Highlight any volunteer work you have undertaken to showcase your enthusiasm and dedication.

Additional Sections: Incorporate language skills, personal projects, or other pertinent activities in this section.

And to make your resume even better, keep these points in mind:

Tailor your resume to the job or internship. Customize your resume based on the specific requirements of the position you are applying for. Utilize keywords from the job description to illustrate how your skills and experiences closely match the role's requirements.

Keep it concise and well-organized. Limit your resume to one page, using clear headings, bullet points, and a clean format. Use a professional font and proofread carefully for any errors or typos.

Be honest and accurate. Do not exaggerate your skills or experience.

Include references or a statement of availability. If applicable, provide references, mention your interview availability, or give more information.

Proofread. Check and double-check your resume before submitting it.

Limit it to a single page. Make the content brief and concise so employers can quickly obtain the information that answers, "Why should we hire you?"

Save your resume in PDF format. This maintains consistent formatting across different platforms.

Meanwhile, here's a sample template you can use as a guide in creating your own:

SERENE COTILLARD

A highly motivated and creative students seeking a social media manager position to ultilize my passion for digital marketing and social media platforms. Eager to contribute my strong organization skills, attention to details, and knowledge of effectively engaging with their target audience.

SKILLS

- Proficient in social media platforms such as Tiktok, Instagram, LinkedIn and Twitter
- Familiarity with social media management tools and analytics
- Strong written and verbal communication skills
- Creative thinking and ability to generate engaging content
- Graphic design skills using Adobe Photoshop, Illustrator, and Canva
- Excellent organizational skills and ability to meet deadlines
- Detail-oriented and strong attention to grammar and spelling

📞 123-456-7890

✉️ serenecotillard00@gmail.com

🌐 www.itsserene.com

in linkedin.com/in/serene_cottilard00

📍 123 Anywhere St. Any City

EXPERIENCE

- Part-time Freelance Graphic Designer
- Fiverr (20xx-20xx)

HOBBIES AND INTERESTS

- Content creation for my TikTok, YouTube, Instagram, and Facebook accounts
- Photography
- Writing and blogging
- Traveling
- Reading

OTHER ACTIVITIES

- President, Social Media Club at Hillside High School
- Member, Student Council
- Volunteer, Community Service Club

EDUCATION

- Junior at Hillside High School with A's and B's
- Taking Spanish, Language Arts, Visual Arts, Creative Writing, and Computer Science

Writing Application Letters

A high school student's cover letter showcases skills and relevant experience, expressing interest to potential employers. It focuses on career goals rather than prior job experience, typically spanning three paragraphs with a greeting and closing line.

A carefully-crafted cover letter can set you apart and positively impact the employer. To accomplish this objective, remember these essential aspects when creating your cover letter:

Contact Information: Start your cover letter by placing your name, phone contact, address, and email address in the header section. Also, mention the date of writing and the employer's contact information, if available.

Salutation: It is best to address the letter to a specific individual, but if you don't have a contact name, use a professional greeting like "Dear Hiring Professional," "Dear Recruiting Team," or "Dear [Company Name]."

Introduction: Begin the letter by introducing yourself and clearly stating the position you seek in your application. Mention how you came across the job opening or any personal connection with the company.

Body Paragraphs: In the letter's main body, highlight your relevant qualifications and experiences. Focus on the skills and achievements that make you a strong fit for the position. Provide specific examples demonstrating your abilities and how they align with the job requirements.

Personalize and Customize: Tailor your cover letter to each company you apply to. Take time to research the company's needs, values, and culture. This will demonstrate your interest in and suitability for the organization.

Key Accomplishments: Highlight specific accomplishments or projects exemplifying your skills and abilities. Quantify your achievements whenever possible to provide concrete evidence of your capabilities.

Skills and Attributes: Emphasize the skills and attributes that are most relevant to the job. This can include technical skills, soft skills, or specific industry knowledge that you possess.

Closing: Conclude the letter by conveying your excitement about the prospect of making a meaningful impact on the company. Express gratitude for the employer's time and consideration, and end with a professional closing, such as "Sincerely" or "Best regards," followed by your name.

Signature: Sign your name if you submit a physical copy of the letter. If you're submitting it electronically, you can include a typed signature.

Remember to keep your cover letter concise, typically around one page. Maintain a consistently professional and formal tone throughout the letter, and carefully proofread it for errors or typos.

Elevate your resume by leveraging your cover letter to present additional details about your qualifications, skillfully demonstrating why you are the most suitable candidate for the job.

Meanwhile, you can format your cover letter like this:

Serene Cotillard
Phone: 123-456-7890
Email: serenecotillard00@gmail.com
LinkedIn: linkedin.com/in/serene_cottilard00
Website: www.itsserene.com

A highly motivated and creative student seeking a social media manager position to utilize my passion for digital marketing and social media platforms. Eager to contribute my strong organizational skills, attention to detail, and knowledge of effectively engaging with their target audience.

Education

- Junior at Hillside High School with A's and B's
- Taking Spanish, Language Arts, Visual Arts, Creative Writing, and
- Computer Science

Skills

- Proficient in social media platforms such as Tiktok, Instagram,
- LinkedIn, and Twitter
- Familiarity with social media management tools and analytics
- Strong written and verbal communication skills
- Creative thinking and ability to generate engaging content
- Graphic design skills using Adobe Photoshop, Illustrator, and Canva
- Excellent organizational skills and ability to meet deadlines
- Detail-oriented and strong attention to grammar and spelling

Experience

- Part-time Freelance Graphic Designer
- Fiverr (20xx-20xx)

Hobbies and Interests

- Content creation for my TikTok, YouTube, Instagram, and
- Facebook accounts
- Photography
- Writing and blogging
- Traveling
- Reading

Other Activities

- President, Social Media Club at Hillside High School
- Member, Student Council
- Volunteer, Community Service Club

Dressing for Job Interviews

First impressions can make a significant impact on a job interview. One key element that significantly influences creating a favorable initial impression is how you present yourself through your attire. Dressing appropriately for an interview shows professionalism, respect, and attention to detail.

Below are some key suggestions on how you can appropriately dress for—perhaps—your first job interview:

Familiarize Yourself with Different Business Styles

Regarding interview attire, you must be familiar with two standard office dress codes: **business professional** and **business casual**.

Opt for well-fitting suits or sweaters with light-colored, buttoned shirts and tailored slacks, pants, or skirts for a professional business look.

For a business casual look, choose khakis, chinos, or relaxed slacks, paired with dresses or skirts. Avoid jeans and aim to appear slightly more dressed up than the average employee. Complete the look with closed-toe shoes, avoiding athletic footwear.

Business Casual	Business Professional
Blouses or tops	Pant or skirt suits in neutral colors (such as gray, navy, or black)
Sweaters or cardigans	Coordinated blouse or button-down shirt
Dress pants, slacks, or skirts (knee-length or longer)	Conservative accessories and minimal jewelry
Dresses (not too formal or revealing)	Professional handbag or briefcase
Closed-toe shoes or dressy flats	Closed-toe pumps with a moderate heel

Optional: Blazer or tailored jacket	Optional: Hosiery

Get Ideas from the Company Website

Consider this a valuable opportunity to acquaint yourself with the organization and its operations. You can also gain dress code insight through the organization's website. Browse the photos of group or individual employees featured in the "Meet Our Team" or "About Us" sections.

You can also search the company through Google Maps and take note of its interiors. For instance, a workplace with modern and tech-inspired decor generally indicates a business casual dress code, whereas a workplace with luxurious carpets typically suggests a business professional dress code.

Dress According to the Role

Adapt your attire to suit the specific role you are applying for. Tailoring your outfit to align with the position demonstrates an understanding of professional expectations and conveys your commitment to the job. In this guide, we will advise on dressing appropriately for the role, enabling you to make a favorable impression during your job interview.

Choose the Right Outfit for a Virtual Interview

When preparing for an online interview, remember to adhere to the same dress code as you would for an in-person interview. Ensure that your on-camera background is professional and distraction-free. Moreover, dress appropriately from head to toe—yes, including shoes— to project professionalism and boost your confidence during the interview.

Identify What You Should Not Wear

To ensure the focus remains on your face, confidence, and words during an interview, avoiding clothing items that may raise doubt is best. Steer clear of the following attire:

- Loud, distracting prints
- Clothing with printed statements or graphics
- Brightly colored shoes or jackets
- Neon colors (except as subtle accents)

- Sunglasses (unless necessary)
- Loud, distracting jewelry

It's also crucial to prioritize comfort since discomfort can be visible and distracting. Choose fabrics you'll feel comfortable in to avoid unnecessary fidgeting or adjustments during the interview.

The size of one's wallet often gauges success. Mastering the art of budgeting, saving, and investing is a crucial skill set for teenagers. By developing these financial habits early on, teenagers can prepare for a lifetime of financial success and independence.

CHAPTER 6

Nurturing Well-being: Self-Care, Health, Safety, Boundaries, and Growth

---

"Accept yourself, love yourself, and keep moving forward. If you want to fly, you have to give up what weighs you down."

— Roy T. Bennett

Self Care

Self-care refers to individuals' deliberate and conscious activities and practices to promote their physical, mental, and emotional well-being. It involves taking care of oneself and prioritizing personal health and happiness.

Self-care can involve getting enough sleep, eating a nutritious diet, exercising regularly, and maintaining good hygiene. It also includes activities that promote relaxation and stress reduction, such as practicing mindfulness, meditating, taking breaks, and engaging in hobbies or activities that bring joy and fulfillment. Other forms of self-care may involve:

- Setting boundaries.
- Saying no when necessary.
- Seeking support from friends or professionals.
- Practicing self-compassion and self-acceptance.

The purpose of self-care is to ensure that individuals nurture and maintain their overall well-being. People can better manage stress, prevent burnout, and enhance their quality of life by dedicating time and attention to overall well-being. Self-care is essential for maintaining balance, resilience, and self-awareness, and it can contribute to improved productivity, relationships, and overall happiness.

How to Make Doctor Appointments

To make a doctor's appointment, you can follow these steps:

1. **Identify the type of doctor you need:** Determine the specific type of doctor you need to see based on your symptoms or medical condition. It could be a primary care physician, specialist, or a particular department in a hospital.

2. **Choose a doctor or medical facility:** Research and select a doctor or medical facility that meets your requirements. You can ask friends, family, or insurance providers for recommendations. Consider factors such as location, credentials, experience, and patient reviews.

3. **Contact the doctor's office:** Call them during their working hours. Their contact information is available via their physical offices or website, if any. Alternatively, some doctors may offer online appointment scheduling through their websites.

4. Provide necessary information: When you call, be prepared to provide personal information.

5. **Schedule the appointment:** Request a suitable date and time for your work. The receptionist may offer you available options or try to accommodate your preferences. If you have flexibility, it may be easier to get an appointment sooner.

6. **Confirm appointment details:** Confirm the date, time, and any specific instructions for your appointment, such as fasting requirements or paperwork to bring. You may also inquire about any co-pays or fees associated with the visit.

7. **Prepare for the appointment**: Note the details and set reminders if necessary. Gather any relevant medical records, test results, or documentation the doctor may need to review. Make ready a list of questions you can ask during the appointment.

8. **Attend the appointment:** Arrive at the doctor's office on time or a few minutes early. Bring your identification, insurance card, and any required paperwork. They usually ask about your medical history on your first visit.

The process may differ depending on the doctor's office and healthcare system you are dealing with.

When to See an OBGYN

Girls typically need to start seeing a gynecologist between 13 and 15 or when they become sexually active, whichever comes first. You must establish a relationship with your gynecologist to ensure your reproductive health and receive appropriate medical care. But the exact timing may vary depending on individual circumstances, such as personal health concerns or family medical history. Consult with a healthcare professional or primary care physician to determine the appropriate age for you to start seeing a gynecologist.

When to See a Dentist

See the dentist regularly for routine checkups and cleanings is generally recommended. The American Dental Association (ADA) suggests you should have your oral checkup every six months for preventive care (Rosenfeld, 2023). However, the frequency of dental visits may differ according to your need and oral health conditions.

In addition to regular check-ups, you should see a dentist if you experience any dental problems or concerns. Examples include tooth pain, gum bleeding or swelling, loose teeth, mouth sores, jaw pain, or any unusual changes in your oral health.

However, note that these recommendations are general guidelines, and you should consult your dentist for personal advice. They may recommend more frequent visits or particular treatments based on your dental history and current oral health status.

How to Prepare for a Yearly Physical Checkup

Here are ways to help you get ready for your annual physical checkup:

1. **Schedule your appointment.** To have enough time for preparation, schedule it in advance to give you enough time for preparation.

2. **List down your concerns.** Write down any health concerns, such as unusual symptoms or changes in your health. It will help you remember to discuss them with your doctor.

3. **Prepare your medical history.** List any past surgeries, illnesses, or chronic conditions you have had. Include also in your list any medications or supplements you're currently taking.

4. **Review your lifestyle habits.** Consider your diet, exercise routine, sleep patterns, stress levels, and other lifestyle habits that may impact your health. Be prepared to discuss these with your doctor.

5. **Bring your insurance card.** Bring your insurance card and any other necessary documentation with you to your appointment.

6. **Dress appropriately.** To make it easy for your doctor to examine the necessary areas of your body, it's best to wear comfortable, loose-fitting clothing.

7. **Follow any specific instructions.** If your doctor has given you detailed instructions, such as fasting before your appointment or avoiding certain foods, follow them closely.

Remember, your annual physical check-up is an opportunity to discuss any health concerns and take proactive steps to maintain your overall health and well-being. Taking proactive measures in your healthcare can help ensure a successful and productive visit with your doctor.

How to be Safe While Alone

Being safe alone is vital for everyone, regardless of age or gender. As a teenage girl, there are several steps to ensure your safety. Here are some tips:

1. **Trust your instincts.** Your intuition is a powerful tool. If your gut alerts you on something not right or unsafe, remove yourself from that situation or seek help immediately.

2. **Plan.** Whenever you go out alone, let someone know where you're going, who you'll be with, and when you expect to return. Be sure to share this with someone close to you. Consider using location-sharing apps or features on your phone to keep someone informed about your whereabouts.

3. **Stay aware of your surroundings.** Pay attention to your environment and avoid distractions like excessive phone use or wearing headphones that prevent you from hearing what's happening around you. Being aware can help you detect any potential dangers.

4. Stick to well-lit and populated areas. Whenever possible, stay in well-lit areas with plenty of people around. Avoid isolated or dimly lit places, especially at night.

5. **Use transportation wisely.** If you're using public transport, try to stay in well-populated areas near the driver or with security cameras. If you're taking a taxi or ride-sharing service, check the driver's identity and verify

that the vehicle matches the one indicated in the app before getting in.

6. **Be cautious with personal information.** Social media is where you can divulge only a little personal information. Know who can access your data.

7. **Be prepared for emergencies.** Keep your phone charged and accessible at all times. Memorize emergency phone numbers, such as those for the police, your parents, and trusted adults. Consider taking a self-defense class to gain some basic skills and confidence.

8. **Trustworthy companions.** Try to be with someone when going somewhere. Having someone with you can deter potential threats.

9. **Lock doors and windows.** Securely lock doors and windows when left alone at home. If you're expecting someone, verify their identity before opening the door.

10. **Build a support network.** Cultivate relationships with trusted adults, such as family members, teachers, or mentors, who can provide guidance, advice, and support when needed.

Personal safety is a priority, and taking these precautions to reduce risks is crucial. Stay informed, be vigilant, and trust your instincts.

Safety Tips When Walking Alone at Night

Walking alone at night can feel intimidating, but with some precautions and awareness, you can help ensure your safety.

Safety Tips When Living Alone

Here are some tips for you when walking alone at night:

1. Be mindful of your surroundings. Stay alert and attentive to what's happening around you. Avoid headphones that limit your ability to hear approaching sounds or notice potential hazards.

2. Stick to well-lit areas. Choose well-lit streets, paths, or areas with good visibility whenever possible. Avoid poorly lit or deserted areas, which can make you more vulnerable.

3. Let someone know your plans. Let someone know your intended route and approximate arrival time. If anything unexpected happens, they will be aware of your whereabouts.

4. Walk confidently. Appear confident and purposeful while walking. Walk with a steady pace and maintain good posture. It can deter potential attackers and make you less of a target.

5. Trust your instincts. If you sense danger, trust your gut instincts. If a street or situation gives you a bad feeling, avoiding caution and finding an alternate route or safe place is better.

6. Carry a personal safety device. Consider carrying a whistle, personal alarm, or a self-defense tool like pepper spray (where legally permitted) as a deterrent if needed.

7. Stay visible. Wear reflective or bright-colored clothing to increase your visibility to motorists and passersby.

8. Avoid displaying valuables. Keep expensive jewelry, electronics, or other valuables hidden to minimize the risk of attracting unwanted attention or becoming a target for theft.

9. Avoid confrontations. If you encounter someone who appears suspicious or makes you uncomfortable, trust your instincts and avoid conflicts. Cross the street, change direction, or find a well-populated area.

10. Use well-traveled routes. Stick to busy streets and well-traveled paths rather than taking shortcuts through isolated or unfamiliar areas. The presence of other people can act as a deterrent to potential threats.

Personal safety is a top priority, and it's essential to adapt these tips based on your location, local safety concerns, and personal comfort level.

Respect for Self and Others

How to Show Respect for Others

Showing respect for others as a teenage girl is essential to personal growth and building healthy relationships. These tips here demonstrate respect toward others:

1. **Treat others with kindness:** Give everyone the same level of respect and consideration. Show compassion and empathy towards others, regardless of appearance, beliefs, and background.

2. **Avoid rumor-mongering:** Engaging in gossip can be impolite and harmful. Refrain from spreading rumors that may harm someone's reputation but focus on building positive connections.

3. **Be inclusive and accepting:** Embrace diversity and inclusivity by accepting people for who they are. Respect and appreciate different cultures, perspectives, and identities. Avoid judgment and stereotyping.

4. **Be supportive:** Encourage and support your friends, classmates, and peers in their endeavors. Celebrate their achievements and offer help when they need it. Show genuine care and consideration for their well-being.

5. **Resolve conflicts peacefully:** Disagreements and conflicts are natural, but it's essential to handle them respectfully. Listen to others' perspectives, express your thoughts calmly, and work towards finding a compromise or resolution that respects everyone involved.

6. **Respect different opinions:** People may have differing opinions and beliefs, and it's crucial to respect them, even if you disagree. Engage in constructive conversations that promote understanding rather than arguments or belittlement.

7. **Be a role model for others:** Influence other girls by leading by example, e.g., consistently showing respectful behavior. When you treat others with respect, you inspire them to do the same, and you'll never know the impact it will create in others.

Respect is a two-way street; expecting and demanding respect for yourself is essential. By practicing respect towards others, you contribute to creating a positive environment for everyone around you.

How to Show and Practice Self-Respect

Showing and practicing self-respect is crucial for maintaining healthy self-esteem and building solid relationships with others. Here are some ways to demonstrate and cultivate self-respect:

1. Set clear boundaries: Identify your limits and communicate them assertively to others. Respecting your

boundaries sends a message that your needs and well-being are essential.

2. Exercise self-care: Prioritize activities that nourish and energize you, such as exercising, eating nutritious food, getting enough sleep, engaging in hobbies, and spending time with loved ones. Self-care demonstrates that you value yourself and your overall health.

3. Honor your values: Understand your core values and align with them. When you honor your values, you strengthen your self-respect and create a sense of authenticity.

4. Practice self-compassion: Treat yourself with kindness, understanding, and forgiveness. Embrace your imperfections and learn from your mistakes without harsh self-judgment. Cultivating self-compassion allows you to acknowledge your humanity and nurture a positive relationship with yourself.

5. Stand up for yourself: Assertively express your thoughts, feelings, and needs while respecting others. Avoid being passive or aggressive in your communication style. When you respectfully advocate for yourself, you send a message that your opinions and emotions matter.

6. Surround yourself with positive influences: Choose relationships and environments that uplift and support you. Surrounding yourself with people who respect and value you reinforces your self-respect. Seek out role models and mentors who inspire you and encourage your growth.

7. Celebrate your achievements: Acknowledge and celebrate your accomplishments, both big and small. Recognizing your achievements reinforces your self-worth and boosts self-respect.

8. Practice self-reflection: Regularly reflect on your thoughts, behaviors, and actions. Self-reflection allows you to make adjustments and grow in areas where you can improve.

9. Avoid self-comparison: Focus on your journey and progress rather than comparing yourself to others. Recognize that everyone has unique strengths, weaknesses, and experiences. Embrace your path and celebrate your uniqueness.

10. Prioritize personal growth: Engage in continuous learning and personal development. Set goals and work towards them, whether related to your career, relationships, or

personal interests. Investing in your growth and development shows self-respect.

Self-respect is an ongoing practice that requires patience and self-awareness. Implementing these strategies can cultivate strong self-respect and foster a more fulfilling life.

Personal Hygiene

Importance of Good Personal Hygiene

Good personal hygiene is crucial for maintaining overall health and well-being. It involves practicing habits that promote cleanliness and prevent the spread of germs and diseases. Here are some key reasons why good personal hygiene is essential:

1. **Disease prevention:** Proper hygiene practices, such as regular handwashing, can significantly reduce the risk of infectious diseases. Many illnesses, including colds, flu, and gastrointestinal infections, are caused by germs easily spread through touch or contaminated surfaces. By maintaining good personal hygiene, you can limit these pathogens' transmission and protect yourself and others.

2. **Body odor control:** Maintaining cleanliness helps to prevent unpleasant body odor. Regular bathing, wearing clean clothes, and practicing good oral hygiene can help

eliminate the bacteria and sweat contributing to body odor. It promotes a more pleasant and socially acceptable personal environment.

3. **Skin health:** Good personal hygiene is vital in maintaining healthy skin. Regular bathing removes dirt, sweat, and excess oil can clog pores that may lead to skin problems like acne. Proper skincare, including moisturizing and sun protection, also helps keep the skin in good condition.

4. **Dental health**: Oral hygiene is essential for maintaining healthy teeth and gums—regular brushing, flossing, and mouthwash to prevent cavities and reduce the risk of gum disease. Good dental hygiene promotes a healthy mouth and contributes to overall well-being, as oral health is linked to various systemic conditions.

5. **Psychological well-being:** Good personal hygiene can positively affect mental and emotional well-being. Feeling clean and fresh boosts self-confidence and self-esteem, enhancing overall self-image. Additionally, self-care activities, such as grooming and maintaining personal hygiene routines, can provide a sense of control, relaxation, and comfort.

6. **Social interactions:** Good personal hygiene is essential for maintaining relationships. Good hygiene habits also reduce the risk of spreading contagious diseases, ensuring the well-being of those around you.

Overall, good personal hygiene is essential for maintaining health, preventing the spread of diseases, and promoting overall well-being. It encompasses various practices, including hand washing, bathing, oral care, and cleanliness of clothes and surroundings. Prioritizing your hygiene can lead to a healthier and happier life.

How to Practice Good Personal Hygiene

Maintaining good hygiene practices is essential for everyone, including teenage girls. Here are some hygiene practices that teen girls can follow:

- Shower or bathe regularly for your body to stay clean and fresh. Pay special attention to areas like underarms, genitals, and feet.

- Make sure to wash your hair daily. Use mild shampoo and conditioner suitable for your hair type. Brush your hair gently to remove tangles and avoid excessive heat styling.

- Brush your teeth after each meal using fluoride toothpaste. Remember to clean your tongue as well. Use floss to remove plaque and food particles between your teeth.

- Wash your face regularly. Use a gentle cleanser that won't harm your skin. Use oil-free and non-comedogenic moisturizers to keep your skin hydrated without clogging pores. If you wear makeup, remove it thoroughly before going to bed.

- Menstrual hygiene. Change your sanitary pad, tampon, or menstrual cup regularly (every 4-6 hours) during your period to maintain cleanliness and prevent odor. Wash your hands before and after handling menstrual products.

- Underarm care. Shave or trim underarm hair regularly if desired. Use deodorant or antiperspirant to control body odor and keep your underarms fresh.

- Nail care. Keep your nails clean and neatly trimmed. Avoid biting your nails, as it can introduce bacteria into your mouth. If you wear nail polish, change it periodically and allow your nails to breathe.

- Foot care. Wash your feet daily, especially between the toes. Dry them thoroughly and apply foot powder or antifungal powder if necessary. Wear clean socks and well-fitting shoes to prevent foot odor and infections.

- Clothing hygiene. Change your underwear daily and wear clean clothes. Wash your clothes regularly to remove dirt, sweat, and bacteria. Follow proper washing instructions for different fabrics.

- Hygiene during exercise. Suppose you participate in sports or physical activities, shower, or bathe afterward to remove sweat and bacteria. Wear clean workout clothes and use a fresh towel.

Good hygiene practices are essential for personal cleanliness and overall health and well-being.

When to Ask for Help

Asking for help is a vital skill everyone should develop, regardless of age or gender. As a teenage girl, there may be times when you need assistance or support from others. Here are suggestions on when and how to ask for help:

1. **Identify the need.** Recognize when you require assistance. It could be related to schoolwork, personal challenges, emotional support, or any other aspect of your

life. Understanding your needs is crucial before seeking help.

2. **Choose the right person.** Consider the right person to approach for help. It could be a teacher, parent, family member, friend, counselor, or trusted adult. Consider who is approachable, understanding, and has the knowledge or experience to assist you.

3. **Set the right time and place**. Find a suitable environment for private conversation without distractions. Choose a time when the person you want to talk to is available and likely receptive to your request for help.

4. **Be clear and specific.** Clearly express what you need help with. Be specific about your issue and how the other person can support you. It will help them understand your situation and provide appropriate assistance.

5. **Express your feelings.** When asking for help, you must express your emotions and how the situation affects you. Sharing your feelings so they can help empathize with you and understand the urgency or importance of your request.

6. **Be open and honest.** Be genuine and transparent about your situation. Avoid downplaying or exaggerating the

issue. Sharing truthful information will allow the person helping you to provide accurate guidance or support.

7. **Listen actively.** Once you've asked for help, actively listen to the advice, suggestions, or solutions offered. Show appreciation for their input and take the opportunity to learn from their experience or knowledge.

After receiving help, following up with the person who assisted you is essential. Express your gratitude to let them know that their help counts. If necessary, update them on your progress or any further challenges you may face. Asking for help shows your willingness to seek support and learn from others. It's a strength and not a weakness. People who care for you are always willing to help when needed.

How to Keep Safe in an Emergency or Natural Disaster

Keeping yourself safe in an emergency or natural disaster is crucial for survival. Here is a guide to staying safe in such situations:

1. Stay informed. Stay aware of potential hazards and emergencies in your area. Listen to local news, have a weather radio, or download emergency alert apps to receive updates and warnings.

2. Make a plan. Develop an emergency plan for yourself and your family. Identify safe places during specific disasters, establish communication methods, and create an emergency kit (discussed in the next point).

3. Prepare an emergency kit. Assemble a well-stocked emergency kit with essential supplies. It should include non-perishable food, water, medications, a first aid kit, flashlights, batteries, a portable phone charger, a whistle, a multipurpose tool, a map of your area, cash, and essential documents.

4. Know evacuation routes. Try to familiarize evacuation routes in your area for various emergencies. Plan multiple ways in case some are blocked or unsafe.

5. Communicate with family and neighbors. Establish a communication plan with your family members and inform them of your whereabouts during an emergency. Also, check on your neighbors, especially older people or those with special needs.

6. Shelter in place. At times, it might be safer to stay indoors rather than evacuate. Follow the advice of local authorities and find a secure, windowless room to shelter in place. Use furniture or mattresses for added protection.

7. Stay away from hazards. Keep away from downed power lines, flooded areas, damaged buildings, and unstable structures. Avoid standing near windows during high winds and seek sturdy shelter.

8. Follow emergency instructions. Listen to instructions from emergency officials, law enforcement, or local authorities. Follow evacuation orders, road closures, and other guidelines provided for your safety.

9. Have a backup power source. Consider having alternative power sources like a generator or extra batteries for essential devices. Use them safely and follow the manufacturer's instructions.

10. Learn basic first aid: Learn basic first aid and CPR techniques. These skills can be invaluable in emergencies and potentially save lives.

11. Practice self-care. After an emergency, the best thing to do is take care of yourself. Get enough rest, eat nutritious food, and seek support if needed.

These are general guidelines, and specific situations may require different actions. It's best to follow the advice and instructions from local authorities and emergency professionals in your area.

Self-Reflection

How to Live and Practice Your Values

Living and practicing your values is essential to personal growth and fulfillment. Consider these steps to help you live in alignment with your values:

1. **Identify your core values:** Reflect on what truly matters to you. Consider the principles, beliefs, and qualities that you hold dear. Some typical values include integrity, respect, compassion, honesty, creativity, authenticity, and fairness. Make a list of your top deals.

2. **Prioritize your values:** Once you have a list of your core values, prioritize them based on their importance. Your values will help you understand the most significant

matters in your life and guide your decision-making process.

3. **Understand your values deeply:** Explore what each value means to you personally. Reflect on why these values matter and how they manifest in your life. This understanding will strengthen your commitment to living by them.

4. **Set goals that reflect your values:** When setting goals, ensure they align with your values. For example, if personal growth is a core value, set goals that promote continuous learning and self-improvement. This alignment will give you a sense of purpose and fulfillment.

5. **Align your actions:** Look at your daily activities and behaviors. Are they in line with your values? Consider how you can bring your values into different areas of your life. Try making a conscious effort to align your actions with your values.

6. **Make value-based decisions:** When faced with choices or dilemmas, refer to your core values. Consider how each option aligns with your values and choose the path that resonates with them the most. It will help you make life choices that are authentic to who you are.

7. **Practice self-reflection:** Regularly reflect on your actions and choices. Assess whether you are living in alignment with your values or if areas need improvement. Self-reflection allows you to make adjustments and course corrections along the way.

8. **Surround yourself with like-minded individuals:** Seek relationships and communities that share your values. Engaging with others with similar beliefs will reinforce your commitment to living by your values and support your journey.

9. **Embrace growth and adaptability:** Your values may shift or deepen as you evolve and grow. Be open to exploring new perspectives and adapting your values accordingly. Embracing growth and change will ensure that your values remain relevant and meaningful.

10. **Lead by example:** Finally, strive to be a living embodiment of your values. Demonstrate your values through your actions, words, and interactions with others. Committing to living by your values can inspire and positively influence those around you.

Living and practicing your values is an ongoing process. It requires self-awareness, reflection, and a willingness to make conscious choices. Incorporating your values into daily life can lead to a more purposeful, meaningful, and authentic existence.

Strengths and Weaknesses

Identifying your strengths and weaknesses as a teenage girl is essential for personal growth and self-improvement. Know some steps you can take to know your strengths and weaknesses.

- **Self-Reflection:** Take time for self-reflection and introspection. Be mindful of how you think, feel, and behave in different situations. Reflect on what activities or tasks make you feel confident, energized, and accomplished, as well as those that make you feel uncertain or challenged.

- **Seek Feedback:** Reach out to trusted friends, family members, teachers, or mentors and ask for their honest feedback about your strengths and weaknesses. They can provide valuable insights according to their observations and experiences with you.

- **Assess Your Performance:** Evaluate your performance in different areas of your life, such as academics, extracurricular activities, relationships, and personal interests. Identify patterns of success or areas where you may need improvement.

- **Explore Your Interests:** Engage in various activities and explore different interests. Notice which activities you enjoy and excel at. Your strengths often align with activities that come naturally to you and that you feel passionate about.

- **Take Personality and Strengths Assessments:** Consider taking personality and strengths assessments, such as the Myers-Briggs Type Indicator (MBTI) or the CliftonStrengths assessment. These tools can provide insights into your personality traits and natural talents.

- **Keep a Journal:** Maintain a journal to record your thoughts, experiences, and reflections. It can help you identify patterns, recognize your strengths, and pinpoint areas where you can improve.

- **Acceptance and Appreciation:** Embrace both your strengths and weaknesses without judgment. Accept that everyone has areas where they excel and areas where they struggle. Appreciate your strengths and be patient with yourself as you improve your weaknesses.

- **Set Goals:** When you have identified your strengths and weaknesses, set specific, realistic goals to capitalize on your strengths and address your weaknesses. Create a plan to work towards them.

- **Seek Support and Resources:** Seek resources and support systems to help you enhance your strengths and overcome your weaknesses. It may include teachers, mentors, online courses, books, or workshops to help you develop personally.

- **Practice and Perseverance:** Improvement takes time and effort. Practice regularly and consistently challenge yourself. It will help develop your strengths and allow you to work on your weaknesses. Embrace the process and be persistent in your efforts.

Self-discovery and personal growth are ongoing journeys. Be kind to yourself, celebrate your successes, and embrace opportunities for learning and improvement.

Importance of Goal Setting

Goal setting defines specific, measurable, achievable, relevant, and time-bound objectives or targets an individual, organization, or team aims to achieve. Setting goals maximizes your time, talents, and resources for a more fulfilling and successful life.

Goal setting is critical because it gives you a sense of purpose, motivation, and direction. It helps you measure progress, stay accountable, and promote personal growth. Setting goals maximizes your time, talents, and resources, leading to a happy and successful life.

How to Set Goals

Teens should learn how to set SMART goals. SMART stands for Specific, Measurable, Achievable, Relevant, and Time-bound. It is a framework commonly used to create effective and well-defined goals.

Here's what each letter represents:

Specific: A goal should be clear and straightforward, avoiding vague or general statements. It answers the questions: What exactly do I want to accomplish? Why is it important? Who is involved? Where will it happen?

Measurable: Goals should be measurable to track and evaluate progress. It involves using quantifiable criteria to assess whether the goal has been achieved. It answers questions like: How much? How many? How can I accomplish this goal?

Achievable: A goal should be realistic and attainable within the given circumstances. It considers the individual's abilities, resources, and constraints. It challenges the person without setting them up for failure. It answers the question: Is this goal within my reach?

Relevant: Goals should align with the person's values, interests, and aspirations. They should be meaningful and contribute to personal growth, well-being, or long-term objectives. It answers the question: Does this goal matter to me?

Time-bound: A goal should have a deadline or specific time frame for completion. Setting a target date provides a sense of urgency and helps prioritize tasks. It answers the question: When will I achieve this goal?

By applying the SMART criteria, you can follow these steps to set your goals effectively:

Identify passions and interests: Reflect on your interests, hobbies, and things that bring joy. This self-reflection will help you align goals with your desires, increasing motivation and enjoyment.

Be specific and measurable: Goals should be clear and quantifiable to provide clarity and track progress. Instead of a vague goal like "get better at sports," set a specific target like "improve basketball shooting accuracy by 10%."

Set short-term and long-term goals: You must establish short-term goals (achievable within weeks or months) and long-term (spanning years). Short-term goals provide immediate focus and satisfaction, while long-term goals provide a sense of direction and purpose.

Make goals realistic and attainable: You must set goals that are realistic and attainable, given abilities, resources, and circumstances. Unrealistic goals lead to frustration and disappointment. Challenge yourself but remain within your capabilities.

Break goals into smaller steps: Break down your goals into smaller, manageable steps. This approach makes goals less overwhelming and will enable you to track progress more effectively. Each step should be actionable and have a timeline for completion.

Write down goals and review regularly: Write down your plan and place it where you can always see it to remind you. Regularly review plans to allow realignment, adjustments, and reevaluations and reinforces commitment.

Seek support and accountability: You can benefit from sharing your goals with supportive family members, friends, or mentors, who can provide encouragement and accountability. This support system can offer guidance and motivation and help you stay on track.

Embrace setbacks and learn from failures: Failures are a natural part of goal pursuit. View them as learning and growth potentials rather than setbacks. Adapt, make necessary adjustments, and persevere in facing challenges.

Celebrate achievements: Celebrating milestones and triumphs along the way is essential. Recognize and acknowledge your progress to boost motivation, confidence, and a sense of accomplishment.

Goal setting is personal, and you may have different approaches and priorities. Tailor your goal to your needs and resources.

Accomplishments

How to Recognize and Identify Your Accomplishments

As a teen, recognizing and identifying your achievements is essential for building self-esteem, boosting motivation, and acknowledging your progress. To recognize and remember your achievements, here are some steps to take:

1. **Reflect on your goals:** Start by reflecting on your goals, whether academic, personal, or extracurricular. Consider your progress towards those goals and the milestones you have achieved.

2. **Keep a record:** Keep a record of your accomplishments. It can be a journal, a digital document, or even a dedicated section in your planner or calendar. Write down your achievements as they happen, big or small, so you can look back and see how far you have come.

3. **Focus on personal growth:** Recognize that achievements are not solely based on external recognition or comparison with others. Personal growth and improvement in areas that matter to you are also significant achievements. It can include overcoming fear, improving skills, or developing positive habits.

4. **Celebrate milestones:** Celebrate your milestones and accomplishments. It can be a small treat, a moment of self-appreciation, or sharing the news with loved ones. Acknowledging your achievements supports your sense of accomplishment and motivates you to keep moving forward.

5. **Seek feedback:** Seek feedback from trusted individuals such as teachers, mentors, or family members. They can give you valuable insights and help you recognize achievements you might

overlook. Their perspective can offer a different lens to evaluate your progress.

6. **Embrace a growth mindset:** A growth mindset believes that your abilities and intelligence can be developed through effort and learning. Recognize that hardships and failures are opportunities for growth and learning and do not diminish your overall achievements.

7. Recognize personal values: Consider whether your achievements align with your core values. Personal fulfillment and satisfaction often come from achieving meaningful goals aligned with your core values.

Failures

How to Cope With Failures and Learn From Them

We all experience failure as a normal part of life, and You aren't exempted. But it can be particularly challenging for you, who are still discovering their identities and navigating various responsibilities. Coping with and learning from losses is important to personal growth and resilience. To help you cope with disappointments and turn them into valuable learning experiences, here are possible ways:

1. Acknowledge and accept failure: Understand that everyone experiences loss at some point. Taking failure allows you to move forward and focus on learning from the experience.

2. Allow yourself to feel emotions: Feeling disappointed, frustrated, or upset after experiencing failure is okay. Allow yourself to experience these emotions and healthily process them by engaging in activities that help you relax and recharge.

3. Reframe failure as a learning opportunity: Instead of viewing failure as a negative outcome, reframe it as a chance to learn and grow. Ask yourself what lessons you learned from the experience so that it will be less challenging in the future. Embrace a growth mindset, which focuses on continuous learning and improvement.

4. Set realistic expectations: Sometimes, failures occur because we set unrealistic expectations for ourselves. Be mindful of your goals and ensure they are attainable and aligned with your abilities and circumstances.

5. Practice self-compassion: Love yourself. Treat yourself with kindness and understanding. Avoid self-criticism and negative self-talk, which can hinder your ability to bounce

back from any loss. Everyone makes mistakes, and failure does not define your worth.

6. Seek support: Reach out to supportive friends, family members, or mentors who can offer guidance, encouragement, and perspective. Sharing your experiences with others can provide a fresh outlook and help you realize that you are not alone in facing challenges.

7. Analyze and learn from your failures: Take time to analyze the situation and what to do to improve it. Consider other options and how to apply those options to future endeavors. This process of self-reflection can help you develop resilience and adaptability.

8. Embrace perseverance: Failure should not discourage you from pursuing your goals. Develop resilience by bouncing back from setbacks and staying committed to your aspirations. Remember that success often comes after multiple failures and setbacks.

9. Focus on personal growth: Use failures as opportunities to develop new skills, build character, and expand your knowledge. Seek new challenges, take calculated risks, and step outside your comfort zone. Embrace the idea that

failure is integral to the journey toward personal growth and success.

Remember, failures are not permanent, and they do not define you. By embracing failures as learning experiences and approaching them with resilience and determination, you can transform setbacks into stepping stones toward future accomplishments.

How to Say Yes to Fears

Saying yes to your fears can be essential and beneficial for personal growth and development. Fear often holds us back from pursuing new opportunities and experiences. By saying yes to things that scare us, we confront our fears head-on and challenge ourselves to move beyond our comfort zones. This process allows us to develop resilience and courage, gradually diminishing the power of fear in our lives.

We open ourselves to possibilities when we say yes to new and unfamiliar experiences. We may discover new passions, interests, and talents we were unaware of. Embracing the unknown broadens our horizons, exposes us to different perspectives, and helps us grow.

Every time we face things that scare us and successfully navigate the challenge, our confidence significantly boosts. Each small victory reinforces our belief in our abilities and strengthens our self-esteem. Over time, this increased confidence extends to other areas of our lives, enabling us to take on more significant challenges with a positive mindset.

We expose ourselves to new learning experiences by stepping outside our comfort zones. We acquire new skills, knowledge, and insights that can contribute to personal growth. Saying yes to intimidating opportunities like learning a new language or exploring a new career provides a fertile ground for self-improvement.

Opportunities rarely come knocking on our doors multiple times. By saying yes to things that scare us, we seize the moment and embrace the potential for growth and transformation. Many significant achievements and breakthroughs are born from taking calculated risks and embracing challenges rather than playing it safe and staying within our comfort zones.

Regret often stems from missed opportunities and the "what if" mindset. By saying yes to things that scare us, we minimize the chances of regretting missed opportunities later in life. Even if the outcome isn't what we expected, we can still learn from and grow from the experience, knowing that we gave it our best shot.

It's important to note that saying yes to things that scare you doesn't mean blindly accepting every opportunity that comes your way. It's essential to assess the risks and make informed decisions. However, when you encounter something that scares you but aligns with your values and goals, saying yes can be a transformative step toward personal growth and a more fulfilling life.

How to Say Yes to New Opportunities

Saying "yes" to new opportunities can be incredibly important and beneficial in various aspects of life.

Embracing new opportunities allows you to step out of your comfort zone and challenge yourself. It can give you new skills, acquire knowledge, and gain valuable experiences. By saying "yes," you open yourself to personal growth and development.

New opportunities often come with the potential to explore different perspectives, cultures, and ways of thinking. They enable you to expand your horizons and gain new perspectives. By saying "yes," you expose yourself to diverse ideas and experiences.

Embracing new opportunities involves meeting new people and building relationships. These new connections can be significant for personal and professional growth. By saying "yes" to networking events, conferences, or collaborative projects, you increase your chances of building a supportive network offering guidance, opportunities, and potential partnerships.

Saying "yes" to new opportunities allows you to confront your fears and overcome self-imposed limitations. It encourages you to challenge yourself, take risks, and break free from the constraints holding you back. By embracing opportunities, you build resilience and develop a growth mindset.

Sometimes, saying "yes" to a new opportunity can produce unpredictable and positive results. It might introduce you to new passions, hobbies, or career paths you must consider. Being open to new opportunities creates the potential for exciting and unforeseen developments in your life.

In a professional context, saying "yes" to new opportunities can lead to career advancement and increased job satisfaction. It allows you to demonstrate your willingness to take on challenges, learn new skills, and contribute to your organization or field. It may also open doors to promotions, raises, or career transitions.

Regret often stems from missed opportunities. By saying "yes" to new possibilities, you reduce the chances of looking back regretfully and wondering what could have been. Taking calculated risks and seizing opportunities ensures that you actively shape your life rather than passively let it unfold.

Of course, exercising discernment and considering your circumstances and goals is essential when evaluating new opportunities. Sometimes, Saying " no " is necessary as not all options are suited for you. However, being open to saying "yes" can lead to personal growth, expanded horizons, and a more fulfilling life.

Boundaries

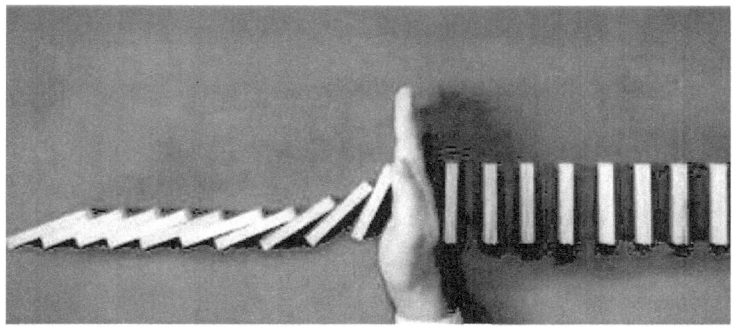

Friends

Sometimes, we have friends who can drain us emotionally, impacting our health and well-being. To avoid it, consider the following steps:

Reflect on your needs: Take some time to reflect on how your friend's behavior affects you. Consider how they are emotionally draining and impacting your mental and emotional health. This self-reflection will help you understand the boundaries you need to set.

1. **Determine your limits:** Identify the boundaries you want to establish with your friend. You may limit your time together, set guidelines for the topics of conversation, and decide how much emotional support you are willing to provide. It's important to know what affects you negatively and what you can't handle.

2. **Communicate openly:** Be open with your friend. Tell them how you feel without any blame. Use "I" statements

to describe how their behavior affects you. For example, say, "I feel overwhelmed when we constantly discuss negative topics, and it's affecting my well-being."

3. **Be specific about boundaries:** Clearly articulate the limit you want to establish. You could say, "I need to limit our discussions about certain topics because they are emotionally draining. Let us focus on more positive or neutral subjects instead."

4. **Reinforce the boundaries:** Consistently reinforce the boundaries you've set. If your friend crosses a border, gently remind them of your discussed limits. Your friend may need time to adjust to the new dynamic, so be patient but firm in maintaining your boundaries.

5. **Take care of yourself:** It's crucial to prioritize self-care when dealing with emotionally draining friends. Engage in activities that help you relax, recharge, and maintain a healthy emotional state. Surround yourself with supportive individuals who uplift you.

6. **Evaluate the friendship:** Assess whether the relationship is healthy and beneficial for you in the long run. Suppose the emotional drain continues despite your efforts to establish boundaries. In that case, consider

whether the friendship is worth maintaining or if it would be healthier to distance yourself from it.

Setting boundaries is practicing self-care and self-respect. It may feel uncomfortable initially, but it's essential for your well-being.

Family

Setting boundaries with family members is essential to maintaining healthy relationships and ensuring well-being. Consider these steps you can take to set boundaries with your family:

1. **Reflect on your needs**: Consider what matters to you before setting boundaries. Consider your emotional, physical, and mental well-being and identify areas where your limitations are crossed or require more space.

2. **Define your boundaries:** Once you clearly understand your needs, identify specific limitations you want to establish. These can vary based on the situation and the family member involved. For example, set boundaries

around privacy, personal space, topics of conversation, or the frequency of visits.

3. **Communicate assertively:** When discussing boundaries with your family, it's important to communicate assertively and respectfully. Pick an appropriate place and time for the conversation and express your needs clearly and directly. Use "I" statements to say how their behavior affects you and avoid blaming or accusing language.

4. **Be consistent:** Consistency is vital when setting and maintaining boundaries. Stick to your limits and enforce them consistently, even if it may be difficult. It sends a clear message to your family members about your expectations.

5. **Practice self-care:** Setting boundaries can sometimes be met with resistance or pushback. It's important to prioritize self-care during this process. Think of your overall well-being, seek support from friends or a therapist, and engage in activities that bring you joy and relaxation.

6. **Offer alternatives:** Sometimes, family members struggle to adjust to new boundaries. To make the

transition smoother, offer alternative ways of connecting or spending time together that align with your limitations. Let's say you need more personal space. Suggest scheduling video calls or audio calls instead of frequent in-person visits.

7. **Maintain firmness:** It's natural for some family members to test or challenge your boundaries, mainly if they were accustomed to different dynamics in the past. Stay firm and assertive in maintaining your boundaries, even if it feels uncomfortable or creates tension temporarily. Respect your own needs and trust that healthier dynamics will develop over time.

Setting boundaries is a continuous process. It's normal for boundaries to evolve and change as circumstances change. Regularly reassess your limits and adjust to ensure they continue serving your well-being.

Significant Others

Setting healthy boundaries with your partner is essential to maintaining a balanced and respectful relationship. Consider taking some steps to establish and communicate healthy boundaries:

1. Reflect on your needs: Identify your needs, values, and limits. Consider what makes you feel comfortable or uncomfortable in the relationship and what you require to maintain a sense of well-being.

2. Communicate openly: Schedule a time to discuss relationship boundaries with your partner. Choose a calm and relaxed environment where you can express your thoughts and feelings without distractions. Communicate

your needs and expectations while allowing your partner to do the same.

3. Be specific: Be clear about acceptable and unacceptable behaviors or actions when discussing boundaries. Clearly define your limits in different areas of the relationship, such as personal space, privacy, time alone, socializing, or financial matters.

4. Use "I" statements: When expressing your boundaries, use "I" statements to avoid sounding accusatory or placing blame. For example, say, "I feel uncomfortable when..." or "I need more space for myself because..." instead of "You always invade my privacy" or "You never give me any space."

5. Active listening: Allow your partner to express their boundaries and concerns. Practice active listening by focusing on what they say without interrupting or making assumptions. Show empathy and validate their feelings to foster mutual understanding.

6. Negotiate and compromise: Relationships involve compromise, so be open to finding a middle ground that respects both partners' boundaries. Look for solutions that are mutually beneficial to both parties and promote a healthy balance in the relationship.

7. Establish consequences: If your boundaries are repeatedly violated, establish effects or discuss potential actions that may need to be taken. Consequences could involve seeking professional help, taking a break, or even ending the relationship if necessary. However, it's essential to consider these measures carefully and only as a last resort.

8. Regular check-ins: Relationships evolve, and boundaries may need to be adjusted over time. Schedule regular check-ins with your partner to reassess your limits and ensure they are still meeting the needs of both individuals.

Setting healthy boundaries is not about controlling or manipulating your partner but establishing mutual respect and trust and maintaining your well-being. Communicating openly, listening actively, and being willing to compromise for the benefit of both partners can be crucial.

Coworkers

Setting workplace boundaries essential to maintaining a healthy work-life balance and ensuring well-being. Here are ways you can take to establish and maintain boundaries at work:

1. Understand your needs: Reflect on your personal and professional goals, priorities, and limitations. Determine what aspects of your work life are important to you and where you feel your boundaries need to be set.

2. Define your boundaries: Clearly define the limits you want to establish at work. It could include specific working hours, limitations on after-hours communication, time for breaks and personal activities, or the type of tasks you're willing to take on.

3. Communicate your boundaries: Once you have identified them, communicate them effectively to your colleagues, superiors, and subordinates. Clearly and assertively express your limits and expectations, making sure others understand what is acceptable and what is not.

4. Be consistent: Consistently uphold the boundaries you have set. It includes adhering to your defined working hours, refraining from excessive overtime, avoiding checking work-related emails or messages during personal time, and declining tasks or responsibilities outside your agreed-upon boundaries.

5. Learn to say no: Practice assertiveness in saying no to requests that conflict with your boundaries. Set realistic expectations and avoid taking on too much work or getting overwhelmed. Politely explain your reasons for declining and suggest alternative solutions or resources if possible.

6. Delegate and prioritize: When appropriate, delegate tasks to others and learn to prioritize your workload effectively. Avoid taking on additional responsibilities that could trespass on your boundaries.

7. Set aside personal time: Dedicate time outside work for personal activities, hobbies, and self-care. Make it a priority to disconnect from work-related matters during these times and focus on recharging and rejuvenating yourself.

8. Use technology wisely: Set boundaries around technology use, such as limiting notifications or setting specific times for checking emails or messages. Consider utilizing productivity apps or tools to help you manage your time and reduce distractions.

9. Seek support if needed: If you're having difficulty setting or maintaining boundaries, don't hesitate to seek help from others -your manager or colleague. They can provide guidance or offer solutions.

Remember that setting boundaries is a continuous process that may require adjustments. Advocating for yourself and maintaining a healthy work-life balance is essential to ensure your overall well-being.

Strangers

Setting boundaries with a

stranger is essential for several reasons. Here are some key reasons why establishing limitations is crucial:

- **Personal Safety:** Boundaries help protect your safety and well-being when interacting with someone you don't know. By clearly defining and communicating your limits, you can ensure that your physical, emotional, and psychological safety is not compromised.

- **Respect and Consent:** Setting boundaries communicates your expectations to others and reinforces the importance of mutual respect and consent. It expresses the right to determine how you want to be treated.

- **Emotional Well-being:** Interacting with strangers can sometimes be uncomfortable or overwhelming, especially if they exhibit inappropriate behavior or invade your personal space. By setting boundaries, you can safeguard your emotional well-being and maintain a sense of control over your own emotions and experiences.

- **Personal Autonomy**: Boundaries allow you to maintain control over your own life and choices. They help you define what is acceptable to you and not, enabling you to choose according to your preferences.

- **Prevention of Manipulation or Exploitation**: Strangers may try to take advantage of others knowingly or unknowingly. By setting boundaries, you are putting limitations, reducing the likelihood of being exploited, manipulated, or coerced into doing something against your will.

- **Communication Skills:** Establishing boundaries with strangers enhances your communication skills. It teaches you to clearly articulate your needs, preferences, and limits, fostering assertiveness and effective communication.

- **Building Healthy Relationships:** Boundaries are essential in all relationships, including those with strangers. Setting boundaries with strangers helps you develop a sense of self-respect and self-worth, which are foundational for establishing healthy relationships in the future.

Setting boundaries is an ongoing process and may differ depending on the person or situation. Trusting your intuition and instincts, listening to your feelings, and assertively communicating your boundaries while being mindful of your well-being is essential.

How and When to Say NO

As a teenage girl, learning to say "no" is an essential skill that can empower life choices and set boundaries that align with your values and well-being. It's easier to say "no" when you:

1. Understand your values and priorities. Determine things that matter to you. Knowing your values and priorities will make it easier to confidently say "no" to things that don't align with them.

2. Can be assertive. When saying "no," be clear, direct, and decisive. Be firm but polite in expressing your decision. Avoid apologizing excessively or using overly apologetic language, as it can weaken your stance.

3. Can you suggest an alternative? If you're declining an invitation or request, consider offering an option you're comfortable with. It can show that you value the relationship and are open to finding alternative solutions.

4. Can Express your thoughts respectfully: Saying "no" doesn't mean being rude or dismissive. Practice empathy with other people's feelings. Acknowledge their request or perspective while firmly expressing your boundaries.

5. Stand your ground: Sometimes, people may pressure or manipulate you into changing your decision. Stay firm and remember that it's okay to say "no" even if others may not agree or understand.

It's your right to set boundaries and choose the best choices. Saying "no" is a valuable skill that will serve you well. Trust yourself and your judgment, and don't be afraid to assert your boundaries.

Hobbies

Why Should I Have a Hobby?

A hobby can bring numerous benefits and enrich your life in various ways. Here are several reasons why having a hobby is beneficial:

Personal fulfillment: Hobbies

provide a source of personal satisfaction and pride. Engaging in activities you enjoy can bring a sense of accomplishment, happiness, and a boost to your overall well-being.

Stress relief: Hobbies can serve as stress relief and relaxation. When you indulge in an activity you love, it helps distract your mind from everyday pressures and worries, allowing you to unwind and recharge.

Skill development: Pursuing a hobby involves acquiring or honing new skills. Whether playing a musical instrument, painting, gardening, or coding, regular practice and improvement can enhance your abilities and broaden your knowledge.

Personal growth and self-discovery: Hobbies offer personal growth and self-discovery opportunities. Exploring different activities can help you discover hidden talents, interests, and passions you might not have known you had, leading to a deeper understanding of yourself.

Social connections: Many hobbies can be enjoyed with others, providing opportunities for social interaction and forming new relationships. Joining clubs, groups, or online communities related to your hobby allows you to connect with like-minded individuals who share your interests.

Mental stimulation: Hobbies stimulate your mind and promote mental agility. Engaging in activities that require problem-solving, creativity, or critical thinking can improve your cognitive abilities and keep your brain active.

Time management and balance: Having a hobby encourages better time management and helps create a healthier work-life balance. It provides a dedicated time for yourself, away from work or other responsibilities, allowing you to prioritize self-care and enjoy your passions.

Increased productivity: Enjoyable free time activities can enhance productivity. Taking breaks to pursue hobbies can improve focus, creativity, and motivation, positively impacting your performance in other areas of life.

Improved well-being: Hobbies contribute to overall well-being by promoting happiness, reducing stress, and fostering a sense of purpose. They add depth and richness to your life, and you enjoy outside daily routines.

Adaptive skills: Hobbies often require adaptability, perseverance, and problem-solving, which can transfer to other areas of your life. The skills you develop through your hobby can be valuable in your personal and professional endeavors.

How Do I Find a Hobby?

Finding a hobby that suits your interests and brings you joy can be exciting. Consider the following to discover a pursuit that resonates with you:

Reflect on your interests and passions: Start by thinking about activities or subjects that interest you, such as things you love doing in your free time, topics you like reading or learning about, or any activities that have caught your attention.

Explore different options: Once you have identified some areas of interest, explore other hobbies within those categories. Research online, read books or articles, and watch videos to better understand various hobbies and what they involve. Look for activities that align with your preferences and excite you.

Try new things: Be bold, and try new activities, even if it means stepping out of your comfort zone. Attend workshops, classes, or introductory sessions related to different hobbies. Many communities and organizations offer trial classes or events that allow you to experience a hobby without committing fully. Experimenting with various activities can help you narrow down your options.

Consider your resources: Think about the resources you have available, such as time, budget, and access to materials or facilities. Some hobbies may require specific equipment or spaces, while others make do with minimal resources. Consider what is feasible and practical for you.

Seek inspiration from others: Talk to friends, family, or colleagues about their hobbies and interests. They might suggest activities you still need to consider or provide insights into hobbies they find enjoyable. Join online communities or forums related to specific hobbies to connect with enthusiasts and gain inspiration.

Start small: Begin with a low-commitment approach. Choose a hobby that only requires a little time or financial investment initially, allowing you to test the waters and see if it resonates with you. Once you feel more confident while gaining experience, you can always delve deeper or explore different hobbies.

Trust your instincts: Attention your gut feelings and intuition. If something sparks curiosity or excitement, give it a try. Don't be discouraged if you don't immediately find the perfect fit— sometimes, it takes time to discover the right hobby.

Evaluate and adjust: Once you've tried a hobby, take some time to evaluate your experience.

1. Assess whether it brings you joy, aligns with your interests, and fits nicely into your lifestyle.

2. If needed, be open to adjusting or exploring new hobbies until you find the right one.

How to Find Time for Your Hobbies

Finding time for hobbies can be challenging in our busy lives, but with some planning and prioritization, you can carve out time for activities you enjoy. Consider these tips to help you find time for your hobbies:

Evaluate your schedule:

1. Look closely at your current schedule and identify pockets of available time.

2. Examine how you allocate your time and identify any activities that may take longer than necessary.

3. Determine areas where you can make adjustments or eliminate time-wasting activities.

Prioritize your hobbies: Determine and prioritize which hobbies are most important to you. Consider the hobbies that bring you joy, fulfillment, or relaxation. You can allocate your time and energy by identifying your top priorities.

Schedule dedicated hobby time:

1. Treat your hobbies as essential appointments by scheduling dedicated time for them in your calendar.

2. Block off specific time slots each week or month to devote to your hobbies.

3. Treat this time as non-negotiable and prioritize it just like any other commitment.

Optimize your daily routine: Look for ways to optimize your daily performance to create more time for hobbies. It could involve waking up earlier, utilizing lunch breaks, or setting aside time before bed for your amusement. Evaluate how you spend your time during the day and identify areas where you can make minor adjustments to accommodate your hobbies.

Eliminate or delegate non-essential tasks: Review your daily duties and responsibilities, and identify any non-essential or low-priority functions that can be eliminated or delegated to create more time for your hobbies. Delegate tasks at work or home that others can handle, freeing up valuable time for your hobbies.

Combine hobbies with other activities: Look for ways to integrate your hobbies into other activities or tasks. For example, if you love artwork or crafts, you can put up a small showroom at home and work on your craft while watching your favorite TV show.

Set boundaries and manage distractions:

1. Establish boundaries to protect your hobby time.

2. Communicate your commitment to your hobbies with those around you, and kindly ask for their support and understanding.

3. Minimize distractions during your dedicated hobby time.

4. Turn off devices, find a quiet space, or use productivity apps that block certain websites or apps.

Be flexible and adaptable: You can never predict what life brings, and there may be times when your schedule allows for less hobby time than you'd like. Be flexible and versatile, and embrace the ebb and flow of life. Find small pockets of time or adjust your hobbies temporarily to fit your current circumstances.

Finding time for hobbies is an ongoing process that requires conscious effort and prioritization. By prioritizing your hobbies, setting aside dedicated time, and proactively managing your schedule, you can create space to enjoy the activities that bring you joy and fulfillment.

Learning life skills is crucial for teen girls' holistic development and empowerment. These skills will equip you to face the challenges and opportunities that come with adulthood, and allow you to make informed decisions, lead fulfilling lives, and contribute positively to your communities.

Your Thoughts Matters!

I hope you thoroughly enjoyed reading *"Life Skills Every Teen Girl Needs: Nurturing Resilience and Independence. Growing Into a Confident Young Woman"*. We put our hearts into creating this book to empower and support teenage girls like you on your journey toward personal growth and success.

Your feedback is valuable to us. We greatly appreciate your thoughts and experiences after reading the book. Did it resonate with you? Did you find the life skills and advice practical and helpful? Did it inspire you to make positive changes in your life? Your review will not only provide us with valuable insights but also help other readers decide if this book is right for them.

We genuinely appreciate your time and thoughts. Thank you in advance for considering sharing your review. Your feedback will be integral to our continuous efforts to improve and serve our readers better.

With gratitude,

Teen Empower

Conclusion

Learning life skills is of paramount importance for teen girls. Life skills are the essential abilities and knowledge that enable individuals to navigate various challenges and succeed personally and professionally. While academic education is undoubtedly crucial, equipping yourself with the practical skills you need to thrive in adulthood is equally essential.

Here are some key reasons why learning life skills is essential for teen girls:

1. **Personal development**: Life skills encompass many abilities, including communication, problem-solving, decision-making, time management, and emotional intelligence. These skills empower you to become more self-aware, confident, and resilient. By developing these competencies, they can effectively handle stress, build healthy relationships, and make informed choices.

2. **Independence and self-sufficiency:** Life skills enable teen girls to become independent and self-sufficient. You can care for yourselves and your living spaces by learning practical skills such as cooking, budgeting, essential home maintenance, and personal hygiene. It fosters a sense of responsibility, self-reliance and readies them for the challenging life ahead as an adult.

3. **Career readiness:** Life skills are directly transferable to the professional realm. Employers highly value skills like teamwork, leadership, problem-solving, and communication. By honing these skills during adolescence, you are better prepared to enter the workforce and excel in your chosen careers. Additionally, life skills education can help them explore different career options and develop a sense of direction and purpose.

4. **Health and well-being:** Life skills education goes beyond academic knowledge and promotes overall health and well-being. By learning about nutrition, exercise, stress management, and mental health, teen girls can develop healthy habits that contribute to their overall well-being. You become more equipped to make informed choices, maintain a balanced lifestyle, and navigate challenges related to your health.

In conclusion, learning life skills is crucial for teen girls' holistic development and empowerment. By acquiring these practical skills, teen girls can navigate the complexities of life with confidence and resilience, setting a strong foundation for a successful and fulfilling life.

References

Indeed. (2021, September). *Top Organizational Skills: Examples and How To Develop Them.* Retrieved May 21, 2023, from https://www.indeed.com/career-advice/career-development/organizational-skills

Multitasking: Switching costs. (2006, March 20). https://www.apa.org. https://www.apa.org/topics/research/multitasking

Rosenfeld, J. (2023, February 20). How Often You Should See the Dentist and What to Expect. *Care Credit.* https://www.carecredit.com/well-u/health-wellness/how-often-dental-exam/#:~:text=other%20dental%20emergencies.-,The%20American%20Dental%20Association%20(ADA)%20recommends%20regular%20dental%20visits%20for,too%20serious%20or%20too%20expensive.&text=While

%20the%20frequency%20of%20visits,every%20six%20m
onths%20is%20recommended.

*Store-Brand vs. Name-Brand Taste-Off - Consumer
Reports.* (n.d.).
https://www.consumerreports.org/cro/magazine/2012/1
0/store-brand-vs-name-brand-taste-off/index.htm

www.ingramcontent.com/pod-product-compliance
Lightning Source LLC
Chambersburg PA
CBHW020440130626
46549CB00001B/230